DATE DUE

JAN 13	.		
1/15/93			
JAN 2 1			
MR 2 9			
APR 1 2			
APR 2 8 199			
MAY 1 8 19			
1994			
3-20-96			
MAR 2 7 19			
FE 27 '0			

Teen Troubles

Teen Troubles

*How to Keep Them
From Becoming Tragedies*

Carolyn McClenahan Wesson

*Walker and Company
New York*

First published in the United States of America in 1988 by the Walker Publishing Company, Inc.

Published simultaneously in Canada by Thomas Allen & Son Canada, Limited, Markham, Ontario.

Library of Congress Cataloging-in-Publication Data

McClenahan, Carolyn.
　Teen troubles.

　Bibliography: p.
　Includes index.
　Summary: Discusses various problems that teenagers face including depression, difficult families, drugs and alcohol, pregnancy, and other crises and advises how to deal with them.
　1. Adolescence—Juvenile literature. 2. Youth—United States—Attitudes—Juvenile literature. 3. Adolescent psychology—Juvenile literature. [1. Conduct of life] I. Title.
HQ796.M386　1988　　305.2'35　　87-23017

ISBN 0-8027-1011-5
ISBN 0-8027-7310-9 (pbk.)

Printed in the United States of America

10 9 8 7 6 5 4 3 2

To Gil, for gracefully leaving me alone to write, correcting my spelling, listening to rewrites, and answering, "Yes," when I asked, "Oooh, don't you just love that sentence?" What more can I ask from a husband?

Thank you,

- Ruth Cavin, for wanting this book written and asking Ann and me to do it.
- Ann Getzoff, for deciding to play and giving me the opportunity to test my wings.
- Kendra Bersamin, for giving me the scoop on publishing.
- Rain Blockley, for helping me learn to write.
- Jenny Vogel, for answering a million questions about teenagers.
- Rosalind, Ward, and Abbe for putting up with a busy, distracted mother.
- Sue Lampson, for consulting in her many areas of expertise.
- Mary Parker Schumacher, special friend and writer, for being truly interested and understanding.
- George and Lorraine Hayes, for passing on their love of words and writing.

Contents

Teen Troubles

Chapter One

Adolescence: Sometimes I'm Up, Sometimes I'm Down

B–E–V–E–R–L–Y*

High school is a place I left with more relief than I left anything else in life, except possibly my first marriage. Actually, it occurs to me now that graduating from high school was my sole preparation for divorce. A rehearsal in walking away and never looking back. Of course, when I left my marriage, I left a man. When I left high school, I left myself—the self-conscious adolescent who inhabited those four years. I never wanted to feel like that person again. To make sure, I threw the friendships out with the memories, knowing that the former would result in an unfortunate encounter with the latter. I spent twenty years crossing streets to avoid people I went to high school with. I once left an entire week's groceries in the supermarket when I realized that I was standing in the checkout line behind our class's basketball princess. I once spent an entire meal in a French restaurant with my hand artfully placed to conceal my face when I realized that my date to the Pigskin Prom was dining at the next table. So when an invitation to my twentieth high school reun-

ion arrived in the mail, I was shocked to find myself excited, even dying to go and see—but what I couldn't imagine.

Delia Ephron
Funny Sauce

*Beverly Hills High School

Comedienne Carol Burnett was having a marvelous time writing her autobiography. She was remembering everything about her childhood, even little details, such as when it rained. Then she started writing about her adolescence. She went blank. She couldn't remember one thing about being fifteen or sixteen or seventeen.

She consulted a psychologist to help her recall those years. He wasn't surprised that she had blocked this period in her life. "Show me somebody who had a terrific adolescence, and I'll show you somebody who either is lying or needs me right now," he told her. In other words, adolescence can be tough.

One way of getting through it is figuring out when things are beyond your control and when they aren't. For instance, you can do little about your developing body, but you can learn many ways to gain control over other parts of your life. That's what this book's about. First, we look at the outside pressures you face and help you understand them. The second part is about ways you can change the inside you—your thoughts and beliefs—so you'll be happier. The third section is devoted to enriching your "people" skills, and that's followed by practical advice about everyday problems.

Growing Up Takes Forever

Adolescence is rough for umpteen reasons. Part of the pain comes from realizing that adulthood and independence are so far off. It takes ten bumpy years to transform yourself from a child into an adult. Unfortunately, you can't always glide through this time like a graceful ice dancer. Instead, you may spend most of these years stumbling back and forth between being a kid and becoming an adult. That's why you sometimes feel so "schizi."

Thirteen-year-old Christine, for instance, was certain something was wrong with her. One day she'd scream at her mother; the next, she'd curl up on the couch and put her head on her mother's lap. Embarrassed about acting so babyish, she was relieved to learn that her behavior was perfectly normal.

Another problem with adolescence is that you're stuck at home, pawing the ground and dying to get out, long before society says you're ready. This conflict comes from your antiquated biological time clock, which is programmed as if you were going to live only until age thirty. Long ago, this was true. Couples had babies at fifteen and then lived another fifteen years or so—time enough to raise them. We now live longer, though, and so our culture says, "Cool it. You're going to live to be about seventy, so never mind the babies. Live at home 'til you're at least eighteen and educated."

Feeling Empty

While you're maturing you may feel empty and somewhat nonexistent at times—as if you were not really there. That happens because you've shed most of your familiar childhood self, but your new self is rather patchy and unfinished. As a result you may feel strange with yourself and uncomfortable being alone. This miserable feeling is normal. Fortunately, it will pass as you get older. It's just one of the many parts of being a teenager, so once you recognize this feeling as normal and know it's not unusual, you can relax. Feeling empty at times means you're making room for your next stage in life.

Reliving Old Hurts

A bunch of other changes occur during adolescence. The sneakiest is the breakdown of your defenses. "Defenses" refer to the way our minds work: they're like barriers that keep unhappy or unacceptable feelings so far away that we don't even know they exist. The combination of your brain adding new cells and your body releasing new hormones causes this temporary weakening of defenses.

When that happens, any leftover sadness from your childhood floats up. You feel depressed, but you don't know why. If your parents divorced, for instance, or one of your parents died when you were a child, you may be feeling some of that hurt all over again. You can read more about this in the next chapter.

Your Body's Going Bananas

As a teen, your body is either changing every which-way or not changing at all. Both stages can be upsetting. Sooner or later, you'll have a growth spurt that lasts about two years. When that happens, you grow about eight inches and put on weight. About one-third of you will be briefly overweight until your weight and height finish increasing and balance out.

New hormones surging through your body raise their own brand of havoc. They are the reason you feel sexy—once in a while, constantly, or some amount in between. Other hormones stir up aggressiveness. Recent studies show that teenage boys and girls with high levels of certain hormones behave differently than teens with lower levels. They express more anger and try to dominate and defy their parents more often. (Those of you who are fighting a lot with your parents can show this paragraph to your parents. "See, it's not me. It's my hormones!")

Finding Nothing's Right

During adolescence your brain gets one-third larger and one pound heavier than when you were a child. With all this new grey matter your thinking changes. In addition to understanding what *is*, you begin thinking about how things *might* be. This new capacity of yours is valuable. You, and others your age, present your parents and grandparents with a fresh view of the world. But this new way of thinking can be disappointing and confusing because you find the world isn't as you thought it was, or how you think it should be. That's partly why you're so critical and angry. Nothing measures up to your standards. Getting used to imperfection is one the biggest tasks of adolescence.

Some teens have a terrible time coming to terms with flaws in their world. A few demonstrate their disappointment and rage by vandalizing the places they believe let them down, like schools and churches. Others deal with their confusion by joining cults that explain life in very simple, black-and-white terms. Looking at the world this way feels safer for some people than learning new points of view.

That's how it was for Rod, a construction worker. He was heartbroken when his marriage of three years ended. Despite his wife's clear declaration that their marriage was kaput, Rod was convinced he could somehow get her back. After two months, when Rod's wife still hadn't returned, he stubbornly refused to face it. His anguish continued.

Months later I ran into him in a market and was astonished at how lighthearted he looked. I told him so, and he declared that he was indeed happy, happier than he'd ever been. He'd moved to a commune in the mountains and become a vegetarian. "That's why I went through the whole thing with Marcie," he explained. "It was supposed to happen so I could become one with the earth and its creatures."

Becoming Your Own Person

Your desire to become an independent, autonomous person is every bit as strong as your sex drive. But satisfying that drive means wrenching yourself away from your parents. This is scary for everyone. Your parents may be afraid you're going to make humungous mistakes that mess up the rest of your life. To protect you they set limits. And, of course, the last thing in the world *you* want is limits, or anything else that cuts into your freedom. So you rebel. If your parents tell you to be home at 12:00, you may come in at 12:05 or 1:05, depending on how restricted you feel.

Slowly taking control of your life is the purpose of adolescence. The question is, how do you go about gaining that control? Begin by choosing issues that involve just you or your territory. It's fair, for instance, that you be able to keep your room as you like it (if you don't share it). It's also reasonable for you to insist that the fine points of your appearance, such as your hair and clothes, be left up to you. Other issues will require a lot of negotiation with your parents. You will find several chapters in this book to help you learn effective ways to do that.

Decisions, Decisions

You've probably been asked dozens of times, "What are you going to do when you finish school?" You may wonder yourself every now and then. It's a hard question to answer. Right now you're focused on today and tomorrow. Who knows about next week or three years from now? Besides, you may be tussling with other decisions at the moment like, should I have sex? What about booze and drugs?

Your grandparents didn't agonize over these issues. They lived under very strict rules that prohibited sex and heavy drinking, so they didn't seriously consider it. And "social" drugs were rarely around. Your parents did face decisions about sex and booze, but not until they were almost through high school or into college.

Today many people your age have to figure out this stuff even before they get to high school. So how can people expect you to figure out your future at the same time? But the way things are set up, all these decisions are thrown on you at once. That's a lot of pressure.

Chapter Two

Society's Confused—and Confusing—Values

Divorce, a very interesting case. A divorce is where two people get out of a marriage. What causes divorces? A very good and familiar question asked by children of divorced parents. I know. I have experience, twice. What I think causes a divorce is stress. Stress from jobs, children, and other affairs.

Divorce hurts, it really hurts. The hurt can make you do dumb and stupid things. When my parents got divorced, I let the hurt take over. That was a big mistake because I got in trouble with the law and I almost flunked school and I felt so bad, I wanted to die.

If you find out ahead of time that your parents are getting a divorce and you want to stop them, don't do anything stupid like jumping off a roof or jumping in front of a car. Instead, just talk to your parents and tell them how you feel. It just might work. It almost did for me.

—Wayne Williams
Age 13
San Jose, California

Because kids your age are committing suicide with grisly regularity, everyone knows *something* is terribly wrong. But, they don't know what the something is. The first thing that comes to mind is drugs: they've got to be the problem. If kids are abusing drugs at astronomical rates and killing themselves off at the highest rate in history, maybe there's a correlation. But experts dash that idea, saying we wouldn't have drug abuse if we didn't have so many troubled kids. If drugs aren't the culprit, then what is? Any why are kids your age so unhappy?

The root cause lies with our society's confused and misleading values. It's hard to see how something so vague sounding could influence *your* everyday life, but it does. The reason you eat steak, for example, rather than beetles and slimy slugs is because our culture says one tastes good and the others are revolting.

Another example is sex. When kids in some Polynesian cultures mature sexually, their village honors them with a ceremony. For the grand finale, the teenager is expected to choose a luscious partner, retire to a special hut and have sex. By contrast, many western cultures are so hopelessly confused about sex that they give their teenagers two contradictory messages: look sexy but, for God's sake, don't be sexual.

So, your culture affects your life. But what is it about our culture that's destroying teenagers? One factor is change. Because you are changing physically, emotionally and socially all at the same time, you desperately need a stable environment around you. Instead, your environment, your culture, changes with each tick of the clock.

Cultural Chaos

Constant change results in confusion and insecurity. You can see the effect of this confusion when you look at one simple bit of behavior—walking down the street. At one time, a man customarily walked on the outside of the sidewalk, nearest the street, when he was with a woman. That way he'd be the one to get hit with the garbage and sewage that people used to hurl out their second-story windows. He'd also, lucky creature, be the one to get wet or dirty if a passing carriage ran its wheels through gutter goop.

Women recently took a look at this custom and said, "Give us a break. That custom is ridiculous and outdated. We can take care of ourselves. Let's not make a big deal about who walks where." Although many women agreed this was logical and fair, not everyone felt comfortable when it got down to the nitty-gritty. It didn't feel right when men walked on the inside and women on the outside. Some women looked at their escorts and secretly thought, "What's the matter with you, you clod. Don't you have any manners?"

Just recently this custom has taken another twist: some people now think that if men walk on the inside, closer to the buildings, they can protect women from any muggers or rapists who might be lurking in dark doorways and alleys. How does anyone know where to walk?

This is just a tiny example of the confusion that saturates our environment. In hundreds of other issues like this, the "rules" are so vague or uncertain that people aren't sure how to act. For example, it's now considered perfectly okay for a girl to call a guy and ask him out on a date. But many girls feel uneasy about the whole deal. Is it *really* okay? What will he think? Isn't it better strategy to wait for him to call? Guys, on the other hand, love it! At long last *they're* the ones who get to be asked, and they're flattered. They also like not having to face rejection.

Such rapidly changing values are the reason you're having a much harder time than your parents and grandparents did when they were teenagers. Society handed them well-marked maps of all the rules they were supposed to follow and those rules stayed constant. That way, young adults knew just what they needed to do to be reasonably happy and successful.

You, on the other hand, are plunging into a society that no longer provides any clear directions about how you can feel content and secure. As a matter of fact, advice about how to be happy is sometimes perfectly lousy. That happens because people have accepted many misleading myths that they try to pass on to you. Here are two of the most destructive.

Myths About Happiness

The first myth says that happiness comes from owning things. While we all get a kick out of having things, especially new things, that lift is like a brief high. It doesn't last very long, and soon we want something more.

Having things does bring us status points, however. That's especially true in junior and senior high where kids walk around with little cash registers in their heads, totaling up the goodies that everyone else has. Kids who have hot cars or designer clothes, for instance, are envied and given higher status than kids who don't. They may not be any happier, though.

Consider Allison's situation. Allison is a beautiful, perfectly tanned blonde who came with her mother for therapy one summer. Allison arrived at each session in exquisite sundresses and matching Italian sandals. On more casual days she'd show up in hundred-dollar designer short-and-top outfits. When I complimented Allison on her beautiful clothes, she thanked me politely but indifferently, saying she had three closets full of clothes at home.

Allison's clothes meant little to her because she had concluded that her mother bought them for her out of guilt. It turned out that her mother loved exactly two people— herself and her new, young husband. She felt very mixed-up about her daughter. She often thought of Allison as a nuisance, but a droplet of motherly pride seeped into her voice when she talked about Allison's spectacular looks.

She brought Allison to therapy because Allison was drinking heavily and staying out all night. Her mother wasn't particularly concerned about Allison's welfare, but she was outraged because Allison's behavior was disrupting her marriage. She eventually solved her problem by shipping Allison off to boarding school in Europe.

So, if you find yourself looking enviously at other kids' clothes or feeling jealous when you hear about their expensive vacations, *don't assume* their lives are wonderful. Granted, there are some lucky kids who come from wealthy, happy homes. But there are many like Allison, who have "everything" but are actually quite unhappy inside.

If you're still wondering whether material things make you happy, try the following exercise: Close your eyes for a minute and think about the things that make you unhappy. What was your answer? Your unhappiness probably had more to do with your feelings about people, or your relationships, or your activities than with things.

The second myth says happiness comes from what you do, not from what you are. It doesn't matter too much what kind of human being you are. The important thing is how fancy your job is and how much money you make.

You've probably already felt some pressure from this myth—either from yourself or from your parents. This is the myth that causes grade school kids to get tense about succeeding in junior high, so they can get onto a college prep track in high school, so they can get into a good college, so they can land a good job and be happy! The following letter to Ann Landers makes just this point.

Dear Ann,
As an upper-middle-class suburban teenager, I hope I can offer some insight into the growing number of

"Never mind the fancy dress and pumpkin coach. Can you get me into Harvard Business School?"

teenage suicides, especially among those who live in the more affluent suburbs. I have known some teenagers who took their own lives and I believe the major causes are as follows:

The pressure to succeed academically and later financially is really heavy. These teens are forced to strive for acceptance to Ivy League schools. If they don't get into Harvard, Yale, Princeton, Brown, Stanford or Amherst, they feel like failures. (It's especially tough if their fathers went to these schools.)

Life in the affluent suburbs is often lonely and depressing. The parents are involved in demanding careers, travel a lot and leave the mothering and fathering to paid help. They almost never do things together as a family.

The fact that the majority of teenage suicides occur in affluent areas such as Westchester County and Long Island rather than in the working and lower middle-class neighborhoods [Author's note: not true] like Brooklyn, Queens and Staten Island must mean that most rich kids, who appear to have everything, enjoy life a lot less than poor kids.

I don't know any of the answers (I'm only 17) but I just thought I'd put some of my thoughts down on paper for whatever they might be worth.

No Name in Winnetka

The culture bombards you with the idea that things and jobs will make you happy, and it's easy to believe that's true. But one of the most important parts of growing up is deciding, for yourself, just what it is that makes you happy. That, naturally, will change many times during your life. Sometimes things will make you happy, and that's fine. But, more often happiness comes from liking yourself and from having good relationships. And, from good times!

Families

In addition to a confusing culture and its misleading myths, the third factor that makes life so rough for kids your age is the condition of your families. One interesting statistic shows that fifty years ago parents and their kids talked to each other between three and four hours a day. Now the average is fourteen and a half minutes. During ten of those minutes, parents issue instructions and check up on the kids: "Don't forget to unload the dishwasher!" or "Have you done your homework yet?"

Today's parents and kids are often too busy to talk together more frequently. Exhausted parents drag in from their jobs at the end of the day wanting "a little peace and quiet." But that's not really possible. Dinner needs cooking, chores need doing, bills need paying, and meetings take people away from home again.

When your parents' day winds down around ten in the evening, they finally have time to talk. But by then, you're often unavailable. You've gone to bed, gone to a friend's house, are watching television, or yakking on the phone. So, you and your parents "miss" each other, day in and day out.

If families don't spend time together, they don't have time to talk. If they don't have time to talk, they may not have good relationships. And while you certainly don't want your parents breathing down your neck, you do need them to be interested in you and available to talk.

Divorce is another major change. If your parents are divorced, or if you have friends whose parents are divorced, you're already familiar with how painful that experience can be for everyone in the family. Teens can face another subtle, and very serious, side effect from their parents' divorce that few people even know about. It's similar to a delayed reaction.

Let's say, for example, that your parents divorced when you were eight years old. At eight you were old enough to understand what was happening, hate it, and also feel powerless to prevent it. You may have begged your parents to stay together; when that didn't work, you eventually gave up, cried some, and felt sad. Within a short time, though, you went back to your normal routine: zooming around the neighborhood, playing with your friends, and not thinking too much about the whole deal.

For the next few years your life went along pretty smoothly. Then adolescence snuck up and you found yourself having all sorts of new and unexpected feelings: rage, lust, and sadness. These feelings come partly from your glands kicking in new hormones, but also from another event. Your defense mechanisms, the invisible shields that block feelings, shrivel up temporarily and all the sadness and hurt you buried during your parent's divorce floats up to the surface.

It isn't as though you find yourself thinking and grieving a lot about the divorce. Instead, the sadness feels like ordinary, everyday depression. Your pain shows up in disguise, and that's why you may feel down with absolutely no idea why. You can't think of anything that's bothering you, but just the same, you feel blue and unsatisfied. Leftover sorrow from childhood, then, is one reason many teenagers are depressed. For many, this sorrow has to do with their parents' divorce.

Other traumas from childhood can cause a delayed reaction, as well. If one of your parents died, it's very likely you will need to face the feelings from that devastating loss all over again. If you moved from an adored neighborhood, or had to move many times in your childhood, you may be feeling unconsciously sad about your lost friendships. Even the death of a beloved pet, now or when you were younger, can cause sadness that you discount because it seems so dumb and childish. But people grow very close to their pets and their deaths can be serious losses.

Our topsy-turvy society, our emphasis on material possessions, and our deteriorating families are three main reasons why adolescence is harder for you than it has been for any other generation. Many believe the combination of these factors is responsible for the spiraling suicide rate among teens. Today's world can no longer provide clear guidelines through the rockiest time of your life. Worse, other people's advice leads to dissatisfaction instead of happiness. And perhaps most important, people in your family may be having such a hard time that they can't offer you the security you so desperately need.

Strange as this may sound, many discouraged people get down on themselves because they're not happy! "What's wrong with me?" they ask disgustedly. "Why can't I be happy like everyone else?" Don't fall into that trap. Remember, the culture isn't making it easy for you. But adolescence isn't terminal and there is plenty of help available. Read on.

Chapter Three

Understanding Your Feelings: Bored, Discouraged, or Depressed?

Because so many teenagers get depressed, you may worry about what kind of shape you're in. Are your moods normal, or are you headed for a depression? What does it mean if you feel nervous a lot? The following descriptions will help you answer these questions and understand what your feelings mean.

The Blahs

People normally have days now and then when they feel listless and bored. Nothing is wrong, but nothing is particularly right, either. It's just a ho-hum, nowhere kind of day. What you have are the blahs, which are nothing to be concerned about. If they drag on for days and weeks, however, you may want to jazz up some part of your life.

Perhaps you're spending too much time alone and need

to get out with friends more often. Or maybe you're in a rut. Do you come home after school and watch the same old TV shows day after day? If so, push yourself to do something different a couple of days a week. Go to the park, fly a kite, cruise downtown, jog, work out, or start a project. Go somewhere you've always been curious about but have never seen.

Prolonged blahs may also mean you're going through a depression. You can read more about other symptoms of depression later in this chapter.

Sadness

For months Reed came home right after school and aimlessly mooched around. He'd drift from one room to the next, always ending up in his bedroom, where he read for a while and then fell asleep. Reed knew he was bored but didn't think anything was really wrong. His parents disagreed and hauled him off to the local shrink. It turned out that Reed was fairly depressed. His best friend had moved away the summer before and Reed hadn't made any new friends to replace him.

Sadness like Reed's is different than the blahs. It's a stronger feeling and usually a reaction to an unhappy event in our lives, or in the life of someone close to us. We can feel sad about many things: the end of a relationship, a friend's unhappiness, a goal we didn't reach, or the death of someone we love. The list is endless; sadness isn't.

Fortunately, sadness has a beginning, middle, and end. It's not supposed to go on and on. If it does, that's probably because you've squashed it down and tried to ignore it so you wouldn't have to feel it. This doesn't work because sadness is a strong and stubborn emotion. It won't be squashed or disappear on its own. Instead, it just hangs around in your body making you feel medium awful all the time. The only way to get rid of it is to let yourself feel it. This often includes talking to someone about your sadness and even crying about it.

How long before you should expect to stop feeling sad depends on your circumstances. If you're sad because of a death, it's normal to hurt about it, on and off, for years. If you're sad about a movie you saw, you should be able to shake it off in a few hours or a day. If you feel sad a lot—say every other day—and have no idea why, for two weeks or more, then its quite possible you're going through some degree of depression.

Disguised Depression

Quite often teenagers feel unhappy and discouraged without being entirely aware of their feelings. They're not aware of these feelings because they're just getting started on a process that takes years to master: noticing feelings and then finding accurate labels for them.

When you were a kid, figuring out your feelings was easy. Your emotions weren't shy or complicated. They just hollered out, "I'm mad," "I'm sad," or "That's not fair!" Feelings were also clear because your world was fairly simple. Things were either black or white, good or bad. When you went to the movies you could tell the good guys from the bad guys at a glance. The good-guy cowboys always wore white, from their silver-spurred boots to their rakishly tilted hats. Even their horses were white. The bad guys wore black, had dark, beady eyes and menacing mustaches. They rode enormous black stallions. You cheered the good guys, booed the bad.

During adolescence you discover that sometimes white can be dirty white, black can be velvety, and a dozen shades of grey emerge in between. Instead of being simple, life becomes complex and occasionally bewildering. Consequently, you focus a lot of your attention on the world outside yourself—noticing it, trying to make sense of it, and reacting to it. Usually when you are around age seventeen or eighteen, however, your attention shifts back inside—to your feelings.

Confusion

Until then, though, you may not have the vaguest idea what you feel, nor what names to give your feelings. Or you may feel many emotions at once,without having time to sort them out. But you do feel—intensely. These big, throbbing feelings are not content to sit around in an easy chair for six or seven years until you give them names. They want action! So you do the best you can. Without even thinking about it, or being aware of it, you express your feelings in your actions. Therapists call this "acting out" your feelings.

Teens, especially those between twelve and seventeen, act out a whole range of feelings, including anger, sadness, hurt, frustration, unhappiness, worry, self-hate, despair, and depression. These feelings aren't picky about how they're expressed. They want out and any old way will do.

Say, for instance, that your mother watches you like a hawk and criticizes your every move. You feel you can't do anything right; nothing pleases her. If you could get in touch with your deepest feelings, you'd find hurt and discouragement. But your surface feelings would be frustration and anger.

Even then, you might not realize the depth of that anger. Instead, you'd only be aware of a milder form, such as, "My mother bugs the hell out me." Consequently, you'd express your anger in fairly mild ways, such as complaining about her to a friend. Or you might even say something snide to her, but do it under your breath.

Your Unconscious to the Rescue

These tame and indirect actions don't make much of a dent in your anger. You're still pissed, so your unconscious mind helps you find other ways to get the rest of your anger out. Not fussy about methods or fairness, it looks around for other outlets.

Your old-biddy algebra teacher looks promising. So does your gym teacher, who nags you all the time about not being dressed properly. Perfect! The gym teacher's critical, your mother's critical—you've got a match.

Next, your unconscious mind goes to work on method. It may decide to annoy your teacher by having you show up to class late. If that doesn't get to her, then maybe whispering while she's talking will work. If you're very angry at your primary target—your mother—your unconscious may pick an especially nasty way to express your feelings in action. It might suggest that you start playing mean jokes on your teacher—whatever it takes to get her upset.

How this process ends usually depends on what happens at home. If your mother eases up on you, your anger will cool down and you'll lay off the gym teacher. If your mother keeps at you, both your hurt and anger will grow and your unconscious will continue expressing your feelings in your actions. In time, you may start believing your mother, thinking her criticisms are justified. That, in turn, can lead to self-hate and depression.

Here's how it worked for one girl.

Patti, a senior, has a secret she feels quite ashamed of. Ever since her sophomore year, she's been having sex with one or two male teachers each year. She has no idea why she does it.

Patti's dad is a millionaire industrialist who has never spent much time with his kids. Patti's two older sisters have reacted to his neglect by rebelling. They flunk classes, smash cars, and ignore curfew. This behavior succeeds in one sense: their father gives them hours and hours of negative, punitive attention when they raise hell.

At an early age, Patti settled on a different tack—to be good and do the best at whatever she did. That way, her father would surely pay attention to her. She got straight A's, kept her room spotless, and never talked back. But it didn't work. Her father never noticed. Puzzled and wounded, she kept repeating to herself, "I'm not that bad, I'm not that bad."

By the time she reached tenth grade, Patti had consciously given up trying to get her father's approval. Unconsciously, though, she was still looking for the warmth and nurturing she so desperately needed. That's why she slept with older men rather than boys her age. Her unconscious mind was trying to find a replacement as close to her father as possible.

If Patti's friends knew what she was up to, they probably wouldn't understand. It was only after several months of therapy that Patti was able to see herself as a deeply discouraged young woman.

Any teenager whose behavior gets way out of line is often acting out his or her unhappiness or depression. Rather than just being weird, wild, or a troublemaker, this person is in pain. The following behaviors can be symptoms of this hidden or masked form of depression:

1. School problems: cutting classes, poor grades, giving teachers a bad time.

2. Promiscuity: being sexual with anyone who's interested.

3. Pregnancy: repeated pregnancies and abortions.

4. Eating problems: overeating, anorexia, and bulimia.

5. Compulsive behaviors: feeling like you *have* to do certain things and can't relax until they're done. Examples are studying the same material many more times than necessary, lying when you don't need to, or keeping your room excessively neat. Rituals such as repeatedly washing your hands, or always getting dressed in the exact same order are also compulsive behaviors.

6. Antagonism to adults: having a constant "chip on your shoulder."

7. Constant anger toward people your age: looking for a fight and finding one.

8. Taking too many risks: driving too fast and wildly.

9. Abusing drugs, including alcohol.

10. Shoplifting and vandalism.

If several of these behavior patterns describe you, you're probably depressed. The more depressed you are, the more symptoms you may have. Also, the more depressed you feel, the more *often* you show symptoms. If you cut a class once a quarter, that isn't serious. If you do it every week, it is. The same is true with other behaviors mentioned above.

If you have a number of these symptoms, it doesn't mean you're a basket case. It just means that you're a person who's suffering and that you need to come to terms with your unhappiness. Try not to feel overwhelmed and hopeless. The rest of this book is about things you can do to feel better and be happier.

Depression

Although most teenagers disguise their depressions, some do not. People in their late teens and early twenties, for instance, are more apt to show their unhappiness in ways similar to adults. Like younger teens, their depressions can come on suddenly or creep in over a period of days or weeks.

In trying to figure out if you're depressed, take time into consideration, just as you did with disguised depression. If you have some of the following symptoms infrequently, you don't need to worry. If you have them for ten days or more, you are probably depressed.

1. You don't like yourself.

2. You put yourself down constantly.

3. You feel helpless to change your life.

4. The future looks bleak to you.

5. Your sleeping patterns have changed. You have a hard time going to sleep or you wake up during the night.

6. Either you don't feel like eating or you overeat.

7. You feel nervous several hours a day.

8. You can't concentrate when you want to.

9. You can't make decisions, even little ones.

10. You feel tired all the time and want to sleep during the day.

11. You don't want to see anyone or talk to anyone.

12. You start watching TV all the time.

13. You feel numb and empty.

14. You don't care about your appearance and don't want to shower.

Remember: If you occasionally have one or two of these symptoms, *don't panic.* It's perfectly normal. If you have several symptoms, day in and day out, that adds up to depression.

If you are going through a depression, you have many alternatives. First, finish reading this book. It will help. The next section provides suggestions about how to get through each day. Doing that—getting through a day—is a cinch when you're feeling okay. In the throes of depression, a day can loom impossibly long.

1. When you feel lousy it's hard getting up in the morning. Yet, doing so makes you feel better. So, the first step out of depression is the step out of bed.

2. Push yourself to get up at your regular time each morning.

3. Once you're up, head for the shower. Turn it on full

blast. Get that water beating on you and stimulating your circulation. If you're hardy, turn the water to cold for a minute. That'll get you tingling.

4. Drag yourself to school, even though you don't want to go. You'll feel more in control of yourself, and of your life, if you stick to your regular schedule. At the end of the school day, praise yourself. You made it through another school day under tough conditions.

5. After school, and on the weekends, try to stay busy. Don't veg out in front of the TV or isolate yourself in your room. Even if you don't feel like talking, you need to be around people and stimulation. If you can't think of things to keep you busy, here are some suggestions: Clean out your closet, plan next season's wardrobe, make a shopping list of things you want to buy. Organize your record or tape collection. Rent a movie for the VCR and plan a special night for yourself—make popcorn or have other food around you enjoy. Polish your skis, fix your bike or car. Work on your tan for a few hours, but only after you've made yourself exercise for half an hour first. Otherwise, it's too much like lying around in bed.

6. Exercise. It's probably one of the most helpful things you can do for your mood. When you exercise vigorously, your body releases chemicals called endorphins. Endorphins actually lift your spirits and give you a natural "high." Run, dance, jog, bicycle, swim, do aerobics, play tennis, racketball, or team sports, or walk as fast as you can.

7. Begin a small, short-term project that appeals to you. Put a puzzle together, build a model, or sew. Make sure your project is something you can easily accomplish and finish. You need successes right now.

8. Keep a diary. It's a wonderful way to express feelings

and get things off your chest. You can also gain perspective on your problems. Be careful, though, where you leave it. Teenagers are notorious for leaving their diaries and private notes out where their concerned parents find them and read them. If you don't want anyone reading your diary, put it in a safe and private place.

9. Schedule things to look forward to. Buy a couple of tickets for a rock concert. Make plans to go to a good movie.

10. Stay away from depressed people. They've lost perspective, too, so you can't be much help to each other.

11. Accept invitations from your friends. If nothing else, they will distract you from your misery for a few hours.

Food

When people are stressed or unhappy they often have strong reactions to food. Some can't stand the sight of it and feel nauseated all the time. Others crave it and pig out. There is a definite connection between our moods and what we eat.

For instance, physicians have found that proteins increase our long-term energy and help us feel more attentive and motivated. Carbohydrates are also an energy source and help reduce stress, ease tension, and make it easier to concentrate. The trick is using the foods from these two groups appropriately.

If you decide you need a lift, then three to four ounces of low-fat protein, such as cottage cheese, low-fat yogurt, fish, or chicken will help. If you want to calm down, one to two ounces of carbohydrates at mealtime may help. It's also recommended that you eat carbohydrates that provide oral gratification. These are foods that require chewing or sucking, such as lollipops, dried fruit rolls, dry cereal, and air-popped popcorn.

If the thought of food nauseates you, but you would like its tranquilizing effects, try liquid carbohydrates—sweetened herbal tea, a soft drink, or hot chocolate.

Drug Therapy

You may have a form of depression that will respond well to antidepressant drugs. Since depression can be caused by chemical imbalances in the brain, it only makes sense to get that balance back in order. That's where drugs come in. They can be extraordinarily helpful in making you feel normal and happy again. Depending on what kind of depression you have, your doctor may prescribe a drug that helps you feel better almost immediately or one that takes about three weeks.

If your therapist or physician recommends drug therapy, don't feel like you must be a real "psycho." Science has discovered that certain depressions are not caused by a person's emotions at all. In other words, it is not a mental problem; it's a physical or chemical problem.

Some depressions are best treated by a combination of drugs and therapy. When this happens, the teenager is given drugs for a few months, until he or she feels significantly better. In the meantime, he or she talks with a therapist about other things that may be making the person unhappy.

Depression and Suicide

The slide from depression into thoughts of suicide can be gradual or abrupt. It depends on what happens in your life and, to some degree, on your age. If you're a younger teen, you tend to go from feeling depressed to feeling suicidal fairly quickly. That's scary for both you and for people who care about you. Even if your slide is more gradual, it's still scary.

The turning point can come when one more awful thing happens in your life: being dumped by a boyfriend or girlfriend, having a failure at school, or having a brush with the police. Because you already feel lousy, you don't think you can stand any more unhappiness, embarrassment, or humiliation. Suicide looks like a way out.

So, if you are already feeling depressed and then something *more* happens, be prepared. Don't let yourself turn this setback into a catastrophe. Keep it in perspective: this latest problem is important, but other parts of your life are equally important. You feel lousy and you've lived through other lousy times, even if they weren't this bad. You learned a lot in the last year, sometimes the hard way. If you hang in there now, even with your pain, your misery will pass.

Above all else, guard against letting yourself act impulsively or quickly. This is hard because your feelings are strong and they want action. But in this instance, tell your suicidal urges to "Shut up!" They do *not* have your best interests in mind. *Suicide is a permanent solution to a temporary problem.*

What if you've got an awful problem and can neither find a solution nor imagine it ever getting better? If this is the case, watch your feelings carefully because you're vulnerable to thoughts of suicide. Although this whole book is directed at helping you solve problems, a word of special advice is needed here. Every problem changes in some way over time. The odds are on your side that whatever is hurting you so much right now will get better. Even if it gets worse over time, *you will change and be better able to deal with it.* You've already experienced this. You've done it before, you are still alive now, and you can do it this time, too.

Warning Signs

When people become seriously suicidal, they give off certain warning signals. If you know these signals you can monitor yourself and know when you're in danger.

1. Your feelings of depression increase. You feel helpless

to change your life and hopeless that anything or anyone can help you.

2. You are angrier than usual, and lash out at people around you.

3. You're preoccupied with thoughts of suicide and can't shake them.

4. You withdraw from friends and family.

5. You cry a lot and can't seem to stop.

6. You take risks you have never taken before.

7. You talk about suicide frequently.

8. You are planning how and when to kill yourself. You are gathering equipment, pills, et cetera.

9. You're giving away your prized possessions to friends and family members.

10. You've attempted suicide before, so you're more likely to do it again.

11. You increase how much you drink or use drugs.

12. You talk about wanting to sleep forever.

13. Killing yourself with someone else sounds romantic, like Romeo and Juliet.

14. You picture your death and funeral, and somehow see yourself being there, witnessing how much people are grieving, missing you.

15. Since hearing of another teen's death, you're preoccupied with that death and the idea of killing yourself.

What To Do

1. Ask for help immediately. Tell your parents or call them if they're at work. Ask them to take you to a therapist.

2. If you can't reach your parents, telephone the operator or 911. People at those numbers will get you immediate help.

3. Call the Suicide Crisis center in your community. Information will have the number.

4. Call a friend and ask him or her to keep talking to you on the phone, or ask your friend to come over immediately.

5. If you can't reach anyone by phone, leave your house so you won't be tempted to go ahead with your suicidal plan. Go to the emergency room of the closest hospital.

6. For most people, the crisis period lasts about ten minutes. This is when they are most likely to carry out their suicide plan. You must get through this ten minutes any way you can. Getting out of the house, on foot, is one way to protect yourself.

7. After your crisis has passed, tell an adult about it. Ask this person to get you counseling.

Chapter Four

Drugs and Booze

People in their teens delight in trying new things, in experimenting. The most alluring experiments are those that involve forbidden things—sex, booze, and drugs. These activities are especially delicious if parents put them off limits. The underlying feeling is that if they say something is bad, it must be good.

Adding temptation are the drug pitches from kids around school. They talk about how good it feels to get high: "You can forget problems, loosen up. The sensations are so intense they're almost like orgasms. Since everyone is doing it, you don't want to be an oddball. And the parties are great. So, why not at least try it? If you don't like it, you don't ever have to do it again. It's no big deal."

If you've been able to resist such seductive invitations, congratulations. Being a risk-taking, learn-from-my-mistakes kind of person, I imagine I would have tried drugs when I was a teenager. But they weren't easy to come by then, and we didn't think they were glamorous. There was this one kid in my junior high who was rumored to use marijuana. We never knew for sure. But just the possibility was so terrifying that my friends and I were actually afraid to look at him! I guess we thought it was catching. Alcohol was around, of course, but it didn't taste particularly good. So that didn't have much appeal. Cigarettes, on the other hand, were definitely sexy and sophisticated. So, that's what we got hooked on, not realizing until too late that it would kill us off at the rate of about 140,000 a year.

Occasional Use

You may think you can avoid addiction if you have just an *occasional* drink, joint, or snort. But even though some people can use a drug once a month and not become addicted, other consequences exist. Sooner or later you may have to lie to your parents about what you're doing. If they find out, you'll blow their trust. Since drug use is illegal, you risk arrest. You also may risk shortchanging your future. Many companies have started asking prospective employees if they've every used drugs. Your honest "yes" answer could keep you from being hired. Yet, if you say "no" and are found out, you'll be fired. It's a no-win situation.

Twenty-one-year-old Amanda is job hunting and confronting this very problem. On the surface, she looks as though she has everything going for her. She finished high school at fifteen and college at nineteen and she speaks three languages. This last year she decided to coast a bit and work at a ski resort in the Colorado rockies. Now she's ready to get a "real" job—one that will challenge her and enable her to use her languages. Her first choices are the foreign service and the CIA, but there's a hitch. Their application forms ask if she's ever used drugs. Amanda has, and she's quite sure she will be disqualified before she ever gets an interview.

The screening of job applicants for past drug use is relatively new. It's hard to say what they'll want to know in a few years. Currently, the FBI will consider applicants who have used marijuana (nothing harder) a maximum of two times.

That's it. While private industry is less uptight than the FBI, the issue is still cause for concern.

When you take street drugs, you face another risk—getting some very bad stuff. Many first-time or infrequent users have had terrifying—and sometimes deadly—experiences. Their drugs were laced with LSD or PCP ("angel dust"). It's kind of like the experience of the unlucky couple who has sex just *one time*, and the girl gets pregnant. It may be unlikely, but it happens.

Finally, getting high may show you a way to escape your problems for a few hours. If the stress in your life increases, you'll want to make sure that your occasional need to escape doesn't become a habit. And then a way of life.

Escalation

Brian, now twenty-six, has been using drugs since he was fourteen. Determined never to use drugs in junior high, his resolve wavered when he started high school. "I was a rookie and a lot more nervous about being accepted. The pressure was more intense: it was something you did to fit in, to be accepted, to be cool."

He and a close friend started by sharing a joint one day after school. Then he and several more friends began smoking pot before football games and school dances. It helped with their nervousness. By eleventh grade, Brian was smoking pot at the beginning of the school day. He and the other students were often excused from their first class, fine arts, to work on their projects. Instead of going to the library, Brian and a friend would jump in Brian's car, drive to the nearby foothills, and smoke a couple of joints. They'd dash back to school in time for second period.

During track season Brian would cut way back on drugs before a competition because he wanted to do well. After meets, however, he and the other guys on the team would party—which meant using pot, mushrooms, acid, peyote, or cocaine. They usually drank a couple of beers at the same time.

How did he feel when he used drugs? "High, euphoric, relaxed . . . it depended on the drug," Brian reported."I didn't think about anything. When you get down to it, we were all trying to escape from something. For me it was problems at home." What kind of problems? Brian sincerely seemed to view them as "normal teenage problems, the usual stuff. Fights with your parents, you know. Nothing much."

When I nudged his memory, other feelings emerged. "I still had a lot of built-up anger about my parents getting divorced in the first place." (He lived with his mother and her boyfriend.) "I didn't feel loved by Dad as much as I wanted. My dad remarried, and he was preoccupied with his new wife and his marriage. I was just kind of there, but distant. I also hated myself because of my disability." When Brian was three years old, two fingers on his right hand were severed in an accident at home. "I also hated my parents for that accident, for letting that happen to me. It was their fault. They should have been supervising me more closely."

When he started college, Brian cut back on drugs and did passably well his freshman year. The next fall, his dad was diagnosed as having cancer, with a slim chance of survival. Brian fell apart—on the inside. Outwardly, he didn't show his fear and heartbreak. Instead, he numbed his feelings with his old standby, drugs. Making good money at his part-time job, he also began snorting coke.

The more he snorted, however, the more Brian went into debt. Bills didn't get paid. Eventually he even owed his pusher. By the time his dad died, Brian was hooked. He was also so disgusted with himself that he said, "Screw this. I'm through." He quit cold turkey and stayed away from coke for two years. Now he has begun using it "recreationally" again. He also drinks two to three beers a day.

Brian has what is called an "addictive personality." This

means he can quickly form addictions to a number of substances. Even though he "kicks" one drug, he soon replaces it with another. He hasn't designed a life, yet, that isn't supported by one drug or another.

Are You Hooked?

The dividing line between drug use and drug abuse, or addiction, is so faint tht it's difficult to know when you've crossed over. The following questions will help you figure out where you stand.

1. Do you use drugs when you're alone?
2. Is it hard for you to turn down a drink, a joint, or a line of coke if it's offered?
3. Do you get high before seeing nonusing friends?
4. Do you need a drink or joint before going to sleep?
5. Do you ever take drugs or alcohol before school?
6. Do you take something during school to get you through the day?
7. Do you become concerned when your stash starts to run out?
8. Do you take anything to improve your performance in school or in sports?
9. Do you feel flat and dull when you aren't using?

If you answered "Yes" to any two questions, you are not an occasional or recreational drug user. You've most likely crossed the line into addiction. The last section of this chapter discusses how to get off drugs and how to get help.

What's Happening?

If you've become addicted to drugs it means you are unhappy about part of your life. Some teenagers are very clear about what's bothering them; others are not. If you fall into the second category—those who aren't sure what's wrong—take some time now to think about it. Perhaps, like Brian, you have leftover hurt or resentment from your childhood. If you notice, when Brian first talked about his problems, he said they were rather ordinary: fights with parents, that kind of thing. As he continued talking, though, old hurts from his childhood surfaced—his accident and his parents' divorce. But those issues weren't on the surface of his mind, at all.

If you can't figure out what's bugging you, enlist the help of a close friend. He or she may see things in your past or current life that are upsetting you. If talking to a friend about such a personal matter sounds risky, consider talking things over with an adult you trust, or a counselor. Another possibility is keeping a diary. Write down your thoughts and feelings for a month or more. Then re-read it and see if there are consistent feelings or problems that come up over and over.

It may be that you know exactly what you're unhappy about, but you have no idea how to change it. Or, you may have tried to change it and gotten nowhere. Feeling discouraged and helpless, you are deliberately numbing your pain through drugs. If you do know what's bothering you, keep reading. The purpose of this book is to help you solve problems. If the book doesn't cut it, seriously consider talking to a counselor. Because once you're in touch with your feelings and know what's bothering you, you've got a head start on solving things.

Overusing drugs is a response to a problem, not a solution. Unfortunately, this particular response is about the worst one you can choose. Only suicide is worse. Drug addiction brings with it a truckload of new problems while it intensifies the old ones.

Drugs Distort Feelings and Behavior

If you are depressed, anxious, or have intense mood swings, you are especially vulnerable to the side effects of alcohol, amphetamines, and cocaine. That's because these drugs play havoc with your moods. They can catapult you to artificial highs and then fling you down to such lows that life seems unbearable. During these intense lows teenagers have killed themselves, not realizing that it was the drugs they were using that made them feel so awful.

Mushrooms, LSD, mescaline, and PCP can have particularly nasty side effects. Terrifying hallucinations, delusions, and paranoia are all possible companions if you have a bad trip. PCP, or angel dust, is an especially potent drug that has triggered both murder and suicide when its users were in the grip of a paranoid reaction. The drug has also caused accidental deaths. For instance, it has made some users feel so miserably hot and uncomfortable that they have tried to cool off by plunging into lakes or the ocean. But, once there, they couldn't judge the distance to safety. Nor could they swim well with drugs in their system, so they drowned.

The side effects of marijuana are subtle and sometimes deadly. If you use it over a long period of time, you may have trouble remembering things, concentrating, and following conversations. It may also diminish your coordination and judgment. That's when it can become fatal. Many teenagers have died because they tried to drive or operate equipment at work while they were stoned.

The short and long term effects of alcohol abuse are pretty well known. But you may not be aware of how it affects your emotions. Alcohol temporarily zaps your defenses, so you feel everything ten times stronger. If you're in a good mood when you start drinking, you'll probably adore everyone around you by the end of the evening. If you were feeling sad when you started, you may end up sobbing uncontrollably. Other times, alcohol pulls a fast one, and dips into your unconscious feelings. That's when you find yourself saying brutally honest, or hurtful, things that make you cringe the next day.

Since alcohol is a depressant you can count on it bringing you down, sooner or later. Sometimes the down will just come in the form of a hangover. When that happens, you feel like hell, but you know it'll pass. Of more concern, is the sense of despair that people sometimes experience. Take Lindy, for instance.

Lindy made a serious suicide attempt after a terrific party. This is what happened. She went to the party, had a few beers, danced, and had a marvelous time. By the time she got home, her high had worn off and depression had moved in. During this alcohol-induced low, she decided that she had reached the pinnacle of good times that evening and her life would never be as good again. She systematically slashed her wrists and ankles with deep, painful cuts.

In therapy, Lindy realized she'd been depressed a long time. But she didn't know that consciously. That's why the down that came from alcohol was so intense. In the grip of alcohol, depressed teenagers may impulsively try to kill themselves. If you are feeling blue and discouraged, it would be a good idea to stay away from alcohol.

And, of course, avoid driving when you've been drinking. It's easy to do something rash and impulsive when you've been drinking. A quick turn of the wheel, and you could be dead. Thousands of teenagers deliberately kill themselves this way. Others kill themselves "accidentally." To help cut down on these tragic and preventable deaths, SADD (Students Against Drunk Driving) have developed a contract for teens to make with their parents. It's an agreement that says no matter what the situation, if you are drunk or need a ride home from a party, your parents will come get you—no questions asked. It's a wonderful, sane solution to a terrible problem. But there are a couple of things to think through before you make such a contract with your parents.

First, if either of your parents drinks too much, or is alcoholic, it doesn't make sense to have them come fetch you. Consider making the contract with a grandparent, aunt, uncle, or nondrinking friend, instead. Second, there may be a time when you're so drunk you can't get your body to function well enough to call your parents. Ask a friend to do it for you. If you are that drunk, another problem might arise. You may be so afraid of your parents' anger that you won't call them. While your worry is understandable, look at it this way. Would you rather have your parents mad at you for two days, or a week, or be dead?

Outgrowing Drugs

If you get off drugs or alcohol, you can increase your chances of living. You can also catch up with other kids and continue your healthy growth. Overturning your addiction is a huge, positive decision but not an easy one. When you turn away from drugs, you leave behind your escape vehicle, and you'll have to find something to replace it. That something can be your determination to face problems rather than avoid them. Here are some steps to help you:

1. Find out what happens to people physically and psychologically when they withdraw from the particular drug you're on. That way you'll know what to expect. Tell your parents or a close friend you're quitting, because you may need someone to help you through the withdrawal. Someone responsible should also know what's happening in case you need medical attention.

2. Get rid of all the junk that you have stashed away. Don't give it away or sell it. Flush it down the toilet.

3. Now get rid of all your drug paraphernalia. Take a hammer and smash your pipes and bongs, spoons, and clips. Break up your stash boxes. If you have any drug jewelry, throw it in the trash, along with those drug magazines.

4. Get on the phone. Start calling your closest friends. Tell them what you just did. Ask them to join you.

Tell them that you'll never get high again and that you have to break away from people who do.

5. Invite them to quit with you. The more friends you can band together, the more fun you'll have doing this. But no matter what, stick to your guns. Avoid kids who continue to use drugs.

6. More than anything else, stay away from drug users and their hangouts. Alcoholics refer to these places as "slippery places" because sliding back into old habits is easy there. Instead, let the pushers know you want no part of them. Keep away from those kids as if they were lepers.

7. Keep busy. Depression thrives on inactivity.

8. Get physically active.

9. Eat well.

10. Reward yourself for your abstinence.

11. Congratulate yourself every hour that you're off drugs. You deserve praise; you're doing hard work.

12. When the withdrawal gets bad, ask yourself, "Can I get through the next ten minutes, the next half hour, or the next hour?"

13. If you have episodes of drifting, flashbacks, or memory loss, don't panic—they're a reaction to withdrawal. Weird feelings improve with time. Just stay away from drugs.

Where to Get Help

If you want to quit drinking or drugs, there are several places you can go for help. Many hospitals and clinics now offer inpatient and outpatient programs for people addicted to drugs and booze. These programs are usually expensive, but your parents' health insurance may cover the costs. If you have been a heavy user for a number of years, you might benefit from both the support and physical care a hospital setting offers.

The most effective program for alcoholics is Alcoholics Anonymous. It is a free, self-help organization that has been helping people for years. AA, as it is called, has meetings in almost every town and city in America. To find out where and when they meet, just call them. They're listed in the phone book under Alcoholics Anonymous.

Chapter Five

You Can Make Yourself Unhappy
By The Way You Think

The young woman was an achiever, a star, no doubt about it. Valedictorian of her high school class, her success continued at North Carolina State University, where she was on the dean's list. If that wasn't enough, she made All-American in track and set a collegiate record in the 10,000 meter race.

No one, least of all Kathy Ormsby, had any premonition how things would turn out that hot, sticky June evening in Indianapolis. Competing in the finals of the women's 10,000 meter, she was running a tight race. Suddenly, she veered off the track, ran out of the stadium and across two city blocks to the fifty-foot-high New York Street bridge. She climbed a high chain-link fence and jumped. Within minutes, her coach found her broken body on the bank below. Hospitalized with multiple spinal fractures, a punctured lung, and a broken rib, Kathy was paralyzed from the waist down and would never walk again. Many months passed before she was able to talk about what happened and why she jumped.

In the vacuum left by Kathy's silence, sports experts speculated about why Kathy had tried to kill herself. One psychologist warned that when young people commit all their total mental, emotional, and physical ability to one pursuit, they risk seeing the world (and themselves) as being totally good or totally bad. Which one depends entirely on how they're performing.

Six months after Kathy's suicide attempt, the *Charlotte Observer* newspaper ran her first interview. She explained that several times in the previous two years she had experienced such severe anxiety while racing that she blacked out and had to withdraw from those races. When the same thing began happening in the Indianapolis race, she explained, "All of a sudden—this is the best way I can tell you about it—I just felt like something snapped inside of me. And I was really angry. And I felt like it was so unfair. All of a sudden, I didn't feel like this was me because I didn't usually have reactions [of anger] like that. That was not a reaction I had as a person, ever.

"I couldn't face the embarrassment, and not knowing what was happening again. I just wanted to run away. . . I was just out of control. I just couldn't face everybody. I felt like I had let everybody down." Looking back, she's convinced she did not plan to commit suicide. A compulsive list maker, she had made notes to herself to buy pizza, and maybe dessert, *after* the race.

Kathy said she has always been exceedingly organized and believed that time was not to be wasted. She planned her days by the hour and kept weekly and monthly notebooks. She was strict not only with her time, but with herself. "I had Kathy's rules and everybody else's rules. I don't really understand why. I never felt I was good at things. I always felt I had to work hard to do well. People would say 'Look at all you've done; how can you be unsure of yourself?' My parents worried about me being a real perfectionist and not ever being able to let go."

After thinking hard about her life, she has now amended one of her rules. "I do think God wants us to do our best," she said. "But I don't think He wants us to be obsessed with that or to do it in such a way that it doesn't leave time for ourselves to enjoy life."

It's easy to see why people who knew the "outside" Kathy—her achievements and successes—were perplexed when they learned she didn't feel good about herself. They couldn't tell that her thoughts and beliefs left her chronically dissatisfied with herself and rarely at peace. Her impossibly high expectations eroded her self-esteem to the point that her whole sense of worth hung on the slender thread of her achievements.

Being Perfect

It's possible that you too may be harming yourself by believing you should be perfect, or that you should at least try to be. Teenagers try to be perfect to please someone, to be acceptable, and to feel loved. That someone may be their self, or it may be their parents or the world in general.

If, for instance, it's your parents that you're trying to please, you have a tough job ahead of you. First, you have to figure out what "perfect" means to them. That's difficult because you cannot read their minds. Even if you could, what they would consider perfect behavior might change. If you play Pony League baseball, your father might want you to hit a homer one inning, but bunt the next. So attempting to be perfect for your parents, or anyone else, is just about impossible.

Even though you can't define precisely what your parents want from you, minute by minute, you may still have a general idea of what they'd consider ideal. They'd probably want you to study, get good grades, be popular, hold a class office, play a sport, keep your room tidy, drive safely, avoid drugs, feed the dog without being reminded, be nice to your younger sister, and happily visit your grandmother on Sunday.

If you met these expectations your parents would be thrilled. But you'd flunk adolescence. During this time of your life, you're supposed to be figuring out what *you* like, what you think is important, and becoming independent. By the time you reach your middle and late teens, the push to be perfect, or to do your best, may come from inside you. Granted, you may have picked up these values from your parents and your environment, but now they feel like part of you.

Expecting yourself to be perfect or to try your best at everything you do is asking too much of yourself. In fact, you are demanding the impossible. No one, *ever*, is perfect at all things at all times. We each have moments of great satisfaction because we've done something well, but those moments don't come all that often. Consistently perfect performance isn't possible.

When you expect perfection, you automatically set up expectations you can't meet. Falling short may trigger a destructive cycle of self-anger, lowered self-esteem, and depression. Some teenagers have grown so angry at themselves for what they considered their failures that they have killed themselves. In fact, they were not failures; they were just less than perfect.

Furthermore, when you try to be perfect to win another person's approval, you set yourself up for constant worry, as Alexandriana did.

Alexandriana fell passionately in love with Jack. After finishing college, they moved in together. They both worked, but Alexandriana wanted to be a "traditional" female. She cooked all the meals, washed the dishes, did the housework, and bought the groceries. After a year, she started having migraine headaches. In therapy she admitted that she was angry that Jack let her do all the work, yet she was reluctant to broach the idea of sharing the chores. She was sure Jack would leave. Insecure, she convinced herself that the only reason Jack stayed with her was because she had become the "perfect" mate. If she quit, why would he stick around?

Alexandriana fell into a common trap—trying to be perfect to be lovable. Besides not being able to be perfect, Alexandriana realized she would never believe Jack loved her, for her, if she didn't stop trying so hard to please and see if he still stuck around. It took her nearly a year to screw up her courage and talk over the situation with Jack. He willingly took over some of the household jobs, and Alex's headaches stopped. Most importantly, Jack didn't split and Alexandriana discovered she was loved for herself.

Both Kathy and Alexandriana learned that having unreasonably high expectations of themselves made them chronically insecure. It took them both a long time to accept their humanness, to be satisfied with themselves when they were average and even less than average. When they learned to change their ways of thinking about themselves, they became a lot happier.

Expressing Anger

Believing that expressing anger is wrong can also lead to unhappiness. Many people have been taught to deliberately and methodically cover up their anger, like a cat covering up its poop. If they can't cover up their nasty feelings, they're instructed to at least be nice about them. That's a bit contradictory.

If you've been brought up in a family that feels this way about anger, you may have adopted some faulty beliefs. For instance, you might believe you'll hurt people's feelings if you get mad at them *out loud*. That's true, their feelings may get hurt. But at least they'll know what you're mad about. If you keep it bottled up, they'll know you're angry at them, but not know why. That is really unkind. You may have also been taught to avoid expressing your anger because it makes waves: you might cause an argument or a fight. Again, that's true, but the alternative is much worse. When people store up anger over a long period of time, they can get so angry at the other person that they just end the relationship. That's far more drastic than an argument. You also may have been told that if you get angry, you might lose control, and hurt someone. Actually, the opposite is true. The more you stuff anger, the angrier you grow, and the more likely you are to "blow" and let someone have it.

Anger is a normal, ordinary emotion. It's just part of the spectrum of feelings: at one end lies indifference; at the other end, love and caring. In between are numerous other emotions, including worry, disappointment, anger, excitement, and joy. Anger is not the ultimate negative feeling, indifference is. Anger means we care enough about someone or something to generate some energy, to get agitated.

When we get angry, we feel it in our bodies. Adrenalin kicks in, our hearts beat fast, we breathe rapidly, and our muscles tighten. Our bodies automatically get ready for a fight. When we try to talk ourselves out of our anger, our bodies don't fully get the message. We do calm down, but our angry energy just hides out, waiting for another opportunity to escape. It's the flip side of the way we feel when we love someone. Our bodies want in on the action in that situation, too. We long to touch that person, stroke, cuddle, and even smell him or her—the works.

Since anger, like love, is a normal feeling, trying to hide it is ridiculous. Instead, you can find effective, positive ways to express it. First, pinpoint what you're angry about. Try to be as specific as possible. Replace vague statements, such as, "My brother's a selfish brat," with more precise descriptions: "My brother's done it again. I was watching Channel 7 and he just walked in and changed it to what *he* wanted." That will help you stay clear about why you're angry.

Second, tell the person you're angry with about your feelings right away. Don't stall and put it off. If you do, you risk talking yourself out of ever saying anything. Third, use an "I" message. "I" messages talk about you and your feelings, not really about the other person. Examples of "I" messages are: "I am angry at you because_____

_____,"

or "Mom, when you _____

_____I felt angry."

A note about "I" messages. They're supposed to talk about your feelings rather than the other person's failings. Using the example above, the "I" message is, "I'm really mad at you because you changed the channel." It would not be appropriate to say, "I'm mad at you because you're a selfish brat." that's a "you" message. A way to remember this is to pretend you're pointing a finger at someone when you're giving an "I" message. If the finger is mostly pointed at yourself, you're giving an authentic "I" message. If your finger's pointed at the other person, wagging away in a scolding fashion, it's not an "I" message, it's a "you creep" message.

It's miserable walking around day after day angry at someone, carrying on little conversations with her in your head. If you express your anger when it comes up, you'll find you feel more relaxed and happy. Expressing anger also goes a long way toward preventing depression. When you feel angry at someone but don't express it, you end up feeling badly about yourself, feeling wimpy or chicken. Over time, your anger at yourself grows, you begin to hate yourself, and wind up depressed.

You may live in a family where showing anger to your parents is considered rude and disrespectful. No matter how nicely you put it, you'll get in trouble, be grounded, or possibly be hit. Since you can't express anger directly, you can get it out in other ways. Anger has a strong physical part, so you may want to let it out in safe, nondestructive, physical ways. Go in your room and beat on your pillow with your fists, thrash your bed with an old tennis racket, do some yard work, play a sport that gives you muscular release. Or, turn on the stereo and dance.

Sometimes you need to go one step farther in settling your anger. Talk it out with friends and adults you trust. Perhaps you can arrange to drop in and talk to your school counselor once a week. Avoid letting your anger build up. When it's stuffed down over a long period of time, you may "blow" at the wrong person, for the wrong reasons. More troubling, your unexpressed anger can bring you down and eventually get you quite depressed.

Some people believe that the best way to handle their anger is to let it out immediately and to hell with the consequences. This can be as limited a way of thinking as never acting angrily. If a quick temper is your style, you may want to find ways to control this, so you don't blast people and regret it later.

Try the following: count slowly to twenty-five before you let yourself say anything. Go into another room for a few minutes to give yourself a chance to calm down before you discuss your anger. Practice expressing your anger by giving "I" messages. You may need to leave your house, take a walk, or do something else safely physical to get the anger out of your system. Jumping in your car when you're upset is not a good idea, however. You may be too mad to pay attention to the road. When you feel you've gotten yourself under control, then talk about it.

Screwy Thinking

Sometimes the way we think about a problem makes it worse than it actually is. Without realizing it, our thoughts can be loaded with exaggerations, generalizations, and plain old screwy thinking. Here's an example. The day before the school dance, you develop a great big pimple on your chin. Horrified, you stare in the mirror, scrutinizing yourself from every angle. The following thoughts run through your mind: "I can't possibly go looking like this; I'd die of embarrassment. Everybody will just want to barf when they look at me. My date won't want to go with someone who looks this awful. I'll come down with the flu and cancel."

In a few short moments you have turned a problem into a catastrophe. With all this screwy thinking, you can easily make a wrong or panicky decision: "I'll cancel." Even if you don't make a bad decision, you suffer another problem with screwy thinking. When you exaggerate, or make a problem larger than it really is, a part of you knows you really don't mean it. But your body doesn't necessarily understand that. It gets all upset and responds as if you meant every word you had thought. Your stomach tightens, your palms sweat, and, first thing you know, you've got a headache.

Because screwy thinking comes naturally and automatically, it's easy to overlook. Stay on guard as much as you can. If you find yourself making problems into disasters, ease up on yourself. Be especially aware of your self-critical thoughts: "I'm no good," "I can't do anything right," and so on. These thoughts pull you down and damage your self-esteem. When you catch yourself thinking like this, stop whatever you're doing and closely examine what you've just thought.

> Screwy thinking: "I'm no good."
>
> Evaluation: This is like saying not one single thing about you is okay. You never have kind thoughts, do good deeds, wish people well. You're a thorough rat. True? Of course not.
>
> Screwy thinking: "I can't do anything right."
>
> Evaluation: You can't part your hair straight, pet your cat right, ever answer a test question correctly. True? No. You do many things well each day. You're just not noticing them.
>
> Screwy thinking: "No one likes me."
>
> Evaluation: Your parents, grandparents, friends,

and every person at school detest you and run for cover when they see you coming. Right? Wrong. It may be that someone whom you value doesn't seem to like you. That could be a more accurate statement. And while that hurts, it's not a catastrophe.

Screwy thinking: "Things will never get better."

Evaluation: Never, at any point in the future, will your life improve in any way. The people and relationships in your life are cast in concrete, so there's no possibility of change. Does this make sense? A more realistic way to express this feeling is to say, "Right now, at this moment, I feel discouraged about my future. I'm afraid it won't change, but I don't know that for sure."

Having read this chapter, you've discovered that it's possible to have power over your problems by putting your expectations, beliefs, and thoughts under a big, thick magnifying glass. That way, you can see how they're influencing your life. In the next chapter, you'll learn still other ways to get more control over your life. You'll learn how to solve problems.

Chapter Six

Solving Problems

When you reach adolescence your problems and worries change. When you were little, you probably worried about things like whether or not you were going to get to stay up late enough to watch your favorite TV program, or whether your parents would let you put up a tent in the backyard. Now you worry about heavier matters. That's happening because you've added new brain cells that enable you to take in all sorts of information and put it together in clusters, called concepts.

You can see how conceptualizing changes your outlook if you compare how two sisters, a seven-year-old and a seventeen-year-old, react to the same problem—their parents having a fight. The seven-year-old feels distressed while it's going on, but when it ends she dashes outside to play with her friends and forgets the whole thing. When her seventeen-year-old sister hears her parents fighting, she remembers that her parents also fought last weekend, realizes that her mother's been looking sad lately, and starts worrying what their fighting *means*. Have her parents stopped loving each other? Are they going to get a divorce? What's going on?

Not only were problems simpler when you were a kid,

but you had all sorts of strong, helpful adults around to help you figure out what to do. But that also changes when you become a teenager. Now adults, especially your parents, are often the last people on earth you want to tell about a problem. You want to figure things out for yourself, and if you get stuck you turn to your friends for help. They become your main consultants. However, while they're wonderfully sympathetic and understanding, many of them are in the same situation as you. They haven't had enough experience or training yet to give you fresh, helpful advice.

There are also times when a problem may be so painful or embarrassing that you don't want to tell *anyone* about it. So you end up struggling with it by yourself. That's what happened to Todd, a fourteen-year-old, who got himself in real trouble last Christmas.

Todd was going around with Marcie, another eighth grader, whom he adored. She dropped hints that she'd love to get this gorgeous peach sweater for Christmas. Todd wanted to get it for her, but he didn't have anywhere near enough money. The closer Christmas got, the more desperate he became. Finally, he shoplifted the sweater.

Store personnel caught him and called his parents. They also called the police, who hauled him off to Juvenile Hall. Todd stayed in the hall just a few hours, but he was traumatized by the experience and horribly embarrassed. Overwhelmed with guilt and humiliation, he hanged himself two days later.

This story sounds freakish and rare, but sadly it isn't. Many teenagers attempt suicide when they get themselves in sticky situations. Their circumstances vary, but for most it's the first time they have had to face a profoundly awful experience. And when they're in the middle of an embarrassing experience, it seems like it will never pass. It's equally impossible to believe that pain or humiliation will also pass. So, in the song "You're Only Human," Billy Loel is saying that sooner or later you'll get your second wind, he means that bad times do pass and you will bounce back. You've just got to ride it out, somehow.

Misery Passes

By the time people are twenty-five or thirty, they know about waiting for their second wind. They've either been hurt in relationships or "blown it" often enough to know that bad times not only pass, but they go through predictable stages:

> Day one is dreadful. That's the day you're hurting so badly that you just want to pull the covers up over your head and hide out in bed all day. You do not want to go to school, answer the phone, or see anyone you know, except maybe your mother.

> By day two you can't stand your grubby body a minute longer, so a shower sounds okay. And maybe a little food. You might even talk to one or two very close friends and tell them how absolutely awful you're feeling. Maybe you could even endure school, or your job, as long as no one looks at you funny or, God forbid, says anything sympathetic.

> By day three, a little anger and a tiny bit of optimism creep in. You realize there's just the slightest chance you're going to live: but only if you never have to see that person again, that pond-life specimen. Or, perish the thought, the people who saw you make such a fool of yourself.

> A week or so later the whole trauma begins to fade. And it's hard to remember exactly why it seemed so excruciating at the time. It's similar to the way you feel after a huge, screaming fight with someone: a week later, you may not even recall what the fight was about, much less the details.

Try Not to Panic

When you're feeling terribly low or acutely embarrassed, like Todd, it's natural to want to do anything you can to end your emotional pain. But you need to grit your teeth and hang on long enough for your defense mechanisms to kick in. Defense mechanisms are little internal shields that protect you from feeling horrible forever.

If Todd had lived long enough his defense mechanisms would have allowed him to begin forgiving himself a little. He also might have gotten mad at the store detective who caught him or perhaps even blamed Marcie for her extravagant taste in clothes. All three responses would have protected him from his unreasonable self-hate.

"Yeah," you might be thinking, "but those are just cop-outs for the illegal thing he did." You'd be right. But cop-outs, also known as rationalizations, help us live with our goofs until we have time to get perspective on what we've done. Then, when our self-hate is under control, we can face our mistakes and learn from them. So, now that you've taken the first step and given yourself some breathing room (literally!), you can move on to step two.

Identify What's Wrong

The second step is defining your problem. That sounds easy enough, but it can be tricky. For instance, Todd could have defined his original problem as: "Marcie wants that peach sweater, and I haven't got enough money to buy it." That would have been a factual statement of his problem, but rarely do we think so coolly or objectively. More often our thoughts run in frantic little circles, like a hamster on a wheel. So Todd's thoughts might have been: "Oh God, I know Marcie wants that sweater a lot and if I don't get it for her she'll be disappointed and probably think I don't like her very much. She might even think I'm just too cheap to buy it for her. If she thinks that, she might even break up with me."

The ideal way to define your problem is to incorporate both the facts and your feelings, but keep them separate. You do that by forcing yourself to state your problem in the most objective, factual way you can. Then you add your feelings and reactions.

Using Todd's situation again, his problem would be defined this way: "I don't have enough money to buy Marcie that peach sweater for Christmas." (Fact) "I want to get her what she wants, and I have a lot of fears about what will happen if I don't." (Feelings) The next step is finding out how accurate your facts, feelings, and assumptions are.

Check Things Out

The only way to check out your "emotional" thinking is to ask questions. If your problem involves another person, you need to talk to him or her and find out what he or she really thinks. There's a saying that might help you remember the trouble that assumptions can cause: "When you assume, you make an ass out of you and me." Dumb-sounding but true.

Let's say, for example, that your best friend hasn't called you in two days. Before you decide that she's mad at you, or that she's dropped you, or that she's lying in bed terminally ill, call her! You can say something simple and neutral sounding like, "I haven't talked to you in a couple of days, how are you?" If she's mad at you or sick, you'll know it in ten seconds.

Brainstorm

Now that you're clear what the problem is, and gotten feedback from anyone else involved, it's time to brainstorm solutions. Most people can see just one or two solutions to a problem, so it's easy to feel stuck. Instead, let your imagination run wild. Then write down every solution you can think of, crazy or realistic. At this point it's very important to just let your ideas flow. You'll evaluate them in the next step.

To see how this step works, let's take a fairly common problem. Fourteen-year-old Chrissie wants to go out with the nineteen-year-old hunk she met at the mall. Her parents say he's too old for her and forbid her to date him. What are her options?

1. See him on the sly.
2. Tell her parents she's going to see him no matter what they think.
3. Ask her parents to meet him first and then decide if she can date him.
4. Ask her parents if she can see him if they go out only in a group with other kids.
5. Tell her parents she made a mistake about his age. He's not nineteen; he's only seventeen!
6. Discuss with her parents what they're afraid of (probably sex) and try to reassure them *it* won't happen.
7. Ask her parents to chaperone their dates.
8. Ask if they can just have at-home dates until they're comfortable with him.
9. Run away together.

Evaluate Your Ideas

Now you're ready to evaluate your ideas. Throw out the obviously dumb ones, like running away together, and then look at the rest. Mull them over. If you need to, rank them from the best idea to the worst.

Your frame of mind when you do this is important. Try

thinking of these solutions as *possibilities*. Think of yourself as a slightly crazed chemist experimenting with all sorts of solutions, not sure yet which one will work, but sticking with it until at least one is successful.

Try Out Your Best Solution

It's now time to try out your solutions. If one idea or the other doesn't work, it's not the end of the world. If Chrissie's parents refuse to discuss what they're worried about, then she can ask her parents if they're at least willing to meet the nineteen-year-old.

Ask for Help

If your ideas don't bring you the outcome you want, at least two more options exist. First, make a list of still other possibilities. Second, share your problem with other people—friends and parents—and get their ideas. Chances are excellent that they'll have other possible solutions. By the way, you can use this step at any time in the problem-solving process. You don't have to wait until the end to discuss things with other people.

To get some practice using this method of solving problems, take a current problem that's bugging you and put it through the preceding steps.

Acknowledge the Brick Wall

Sometimes you can do absolutely nothing to change the outcome of a problem. This is especially true when the situation involves other people who have all the control. If your father drinks too much, for instance, or if your parents are

1. My problem is:

2. If another person is involved, I've checked it out with him or her and he or she says the problem is:

3. Here are all the solutions, but I'm not evaluating them in any way:

4. Now I'll evaluate my ideas, and rank them from best idea to worst:

5. I'll try out my best idea. If it doesn't work, I'll try the next idea and the next and so on.

6. If none of the ideas work, I'll make a whole new list of solutions, or ask a friend, parent or a friend's parent for help.

getting divorced and you want them to stay together, there's very little you can do.

These kinds of problems are extremely frustrating. They also erode your self-esteem because you end up feeling helpless about changing a situation that you hate. That sense of powerlessness in time can make you angry and get you depressed. To avoid this, remind yourself that you didn't cause the problem in the first place. Since you didn't cause it, you cannot be expected to fix it, no matter how much you want to.

So if you can't change the problem, what can you do? How do you handle being dumped by your boyfriend or girlfriend, for instance? With problems like this that involve many kinds of losses—the loss of someone's affection, the loss of a stable home, or the loss of your own power—you need to mourn. This may sound overly dramatic, but allowing yourself to feel a loss is the only way you can eventually accept it, feel okay about it, and not have the pain come back to haunt you later.

When you've been hurt, it's tempting to just put a shine on the whole thing and pretend everything's okay, that you're doing just fine. At least that way, you can keep your pride intact and avoid the anguish of feeling hurt or helpless. But this short-term solution leaves all of your pain stuck in your gut. If you don't get it out, you may do all sorts of self-destructive things to avoid facing your feelings. That will make you feel even crummier in the long run.

Rosalind ran into two major problems during her first year in junior high. Vivacious and curvy, she received the first blow when both the seventh- and eight-grade girls began resenting her popularity with the boys in the school. Out of jealousy, they rejected her. At the same time, her formerly doting father suddenly grew cold and critical. These major losses hurt her deeply and undermined her confidence.

Interestingly, she turned to food to soothe her battered feelings. Over one summer, she gained forty pounds and when school started in September she'd unconsciously "fixed" both problems: the boys were no longer as interested in her and the girls weren't jealous. Her father even warmed up a bit since he was overweight himself and sympathized with her new problem.

If Rosalind had been able to really acknowledge *to herself* how hurt she was, she might have been able to cry out her hurt, or at least unburden it to a friend or a supportive adult.

Instead, she conned herself by pretending everything was fine and ended up with a bigger problem.

Rosalind, like other kids with problems that they haven't really caused, need to let themselves feel very sad about what's happened, to mourn. Many people think mourning just means feeling sad or crying, but it's much more than that. When people mourn, first they feel like they're in shock and that the whole situation is unreal or not really happening. When the shock wears off, they get furious at the person who left them or who hurt them: "How could you do this to me, you rat!"

Then sadness and tears come. Many days, weeks, or months later, mourners start accepting their losses. Although they still hurt sometimes, on the whole they feel okay and optimistic again. Since this can be a painful process, you might try to take a short cut and skip the crying part, for instance. But that doesn't work. Your good feelings can't surface again unless you uncork the sad, hurtful ones first.

In the following chapter you'll find clear guidelines on how to make good decisions that will help you prevent some future problems.

Chapter Seven

Making Good Decisions

One of the most delightful parts of growing up is gaining more control over what happens to you. At long last *you* get to decide all sorts of things about *your* life. You can turn down broccoli, sleep in your clothes, choose your friends, or have a beer. It's all up to you. There's just one little catch that takes some of the fun out of the whole deal. You need to learn how to make a good decision.

A good decision:

1. Fulfills your needs or wants, not someone else's.

2. Won't harm you or another person emotionally or physically.

3. Is realistic and based on fact, rather than on hope, assumptions, or wishful thinking.

4. Has acceptable short- and long-term consequences.

Mastering this skill is a lifelong process, so don't expect to be good at it right away. In fact, you might as well plan on blowing it at least a hundred times before you're forty. Making decisions can be extraordinarily complicated.

Melinda and Her Baby

Sixteen-year-old Melinda faced an extremely difficult decision a few months ago. She was pregnant for the second time in just under a year. The first time, she had an abortion. Now, curled up in the corner of my office couch, she talked about how she had decided to have this baby.

"How do your parents feel about your decision?" I asked.

"My dad's been a lot nicer lately. I guess he knows what I'm going through. He still treats me like I'm five, but the big change has been since I've gotten pregnant. I don't know what he thinks, but he did tell me once not to worry what anyone else said. He said he knew I was doing the right thing and he'd take care of me. I think my dad would probably have me give it up for adoption, but he keeps telling me I'm brave."

"What about your Mom?"

"I don't know. I can't figure her out. All I know is the whole time I'm around her I'm worried she's going to be mad at me. I think my problem is that I want them to be happy about it, and it's not going to be like that. She's really worried that I don't know what I'm getting myself into."

"Do you?"

"I think I know how much work it will be because so many of my acquaintances have been through this. I'll just work until I drop. Kate kept her baby, and she's doing great."

"You got pregnant before, just about a year ago, didn't you? How did you decide what to do then?"

"I made the decision over a period of about fifteen minutes. The person I had been talking to had been through it two times and she told me it was the only thing I could do. I was so scared. Sometimes I really hate it and think it was really stupid [the abortion]. I didn't even think about it. I just had the abortion three or four days later. I felt guilty afterwards. Not because I had sex but because of the abortion. I felt really sad about it, but then again, I think it was the only thing I could do. I know I'll never make my mind up about it."

"About the abortion?"

"Yes. I think abortion is wrong if it's used as a means of birth control. I really believe an unborn baby is living and it has rights, too. I don't think abortion should be used as much as it is."

"What about the father, how's he reacted?"

"He was real understanding and said he'd support me, whatever I decided to do. But he was always talking abortion and I know that's what he wanted me to do. When I finally told Greg what I was going to do, he couldn't believe it and said, 'I can't believe you're doing this to me!' He didn't want me to have the baby, and he never called me again. At first I felt deserted and wavered about having the baby. I felt like I'd do anything for him, do what he wanted, but then I decided that was stupid."

"So how did you decide to have this baby?"

"It's hard to explain. I know I wouldn't be able to go through the whole nine months and then give it up because it would be hard to do that. Then I thought how much better could it be for the kid? Maybe a family could buy the kid lots of things and take him around the world, but how much better would that be than not knowing who his mother was. If it was me, I would have worried why did she do that, didn't she even love me? In my case, I have a family who really cares and who will help me. That will make it a little easier than people who don't have a supportive family."

"So it helps having a supportive family."

"Yeah. If I had to quit school and stop doing things I want to do, it might not be fair to me either. Keeping it would be best for the baby and me. If I gave it up I'd spend every day thinking, what's this kid like? It would be really awful."

"So what are your plans?"

"I'm going to school now and finish, get my diploma in

June. I'm taking cosmetology. It'll take another year by the time I get my license. Then I can go to work."

"What will you do with the baby while you're finishing your training?"

"Mom offered to take care of it until I can pay for daycare, or until it's old enough for daycare. Which is six months. But daycare is so expensive. Or I may have my friend Judy take care of her. She takes care of her sister's two babies and goes to school at night. I'll stay at home until I can pay for my own place. I don't know how much apartments are, but I know they're expensive. And I have to have a car. I'll manage it somehow. I won't even move out of the house for at least a year after the baby's born. I feel bad about it, though, even though they [Melinda's parents] haven't said anything."

"Who have you talked this decision over with?"

"Nobody. Just Mom after I'd pretty much made up my mind. I knew that I really didn't want to get an abortion. I did that last time. Then the decision was to keep the baby or adoption? It took me about three weeks to decide to keep the baby. All day, every day I thought about it. I did talk it over with my friend Judy. She supported me. Then I talked to her sister, who told me more about what it's like to have kids."

"How do you feel about your decision?"

"I don't have any doubts. It was hard to be happy about it at first, but now I think, I know I have enough motivation to work hard and do well."

Decision-making

As you can see, Melinda has had to make a number of staggering decisions that will affect both her and her baby the rest of their lives. Whether you face momentous decisions like hers, or less difficult ones, the process of good decision-making is almost always the same—even when you whip through the steps of an easier decision almost automatically and are less aware of the process.

Step 1. Decide Whether You Have to Decide Right Now.

Sometimes we pressure ourselves, or we allow ourselves to be pressured, to make decisions that can actually wait. Little kids are masters at exerting this pressure. They fly in the front door, dash over to their parents, and say, "Johnny's going to the show with his mom and she said I can go, too. Can I, can I? I gotta know right now. They're leaving in one minute!"

Teenagers are often pushed to make quick decisions, too. What do you say, for instance, when someone unexpectedly pulls out a joint and asks, "Do you want some?" If you can't decide, or don't want to decide right away, *stall*. You may already know some delaying tactics that work well. Many people use phrases such as "I'm not sure" or "Let me think about that a little while longer." Sometimes a quick getaway to the bathroom will give you time to derail someone who's pressuring you.

It also makes sense to put off decisions when you feel sick, overloaded, or depressed. At these times your view of problems may be distorted and your judgment fuzzy. Furthermore, things can look hopeless—as they do when we wake up in the middle of the night and go over and over a problem, and get nowhere. In *Gone with the Wind*, Scarlett O'Hara used this strategy when she was too exhausted or distraught to make good decisions: she'd flutter her sable lashes and utter those famous words, "I can't think about this now. I'll think about it tomorrow." (Unfortunately, Scarlett also used this same technique to hide from anything remotely unpleasant.)

On the other hand, you may have friends who'll do anything to avoid making decisions. Self-critical people are like this. They hate making decisions because they might make a mistake. Timid people also hate making decisions. They don't like calling attention to themselves in any way and loathe hurting people's feelings. As long as they duck making decisions, they don't have to worry about making waves or losing their "nice guy" image.

To summarize: think through whether you need to make a decision immediately. If not, give yourself time to go through all the following steps of good decision-making.

Step 2: List Choices.

If you're agonizing about a decision, it may be tempting just to say, "To hell with it," and make a quick choice to end the misery of indecision. The consequent risk is overlooking good alternatives.

To reach a good decision, take enough time to let your ideas flow. Forget about whether something will work—that's a later step. For now, just think of as many possibilities or solutions as you can. Some people like to write them down. Either way, you will probably feel some relief because you're making progress toward an effective decision.

Melinda felt she had the following choices:

1. Have an abortion.
2. Have the baby.
3. Keep the baby.
4. Give the baby up for adoption.
5. Give the baby to her older sister, who wanted a child.

Step 3: Feel Each Option.

Once you've thought of every option you can, relax and let your feelings about these options surface. Don't work at this. Just go about your ususal routine and let different feelings about your options come and go. It's like trying on five sweaters made of different materials and noticing how each one feels against your skin.

Step 4: Think About Your Choices.

After you've had a chance to note your feelings during a fairly relaxed period, you can begin evaluating your choices on the basis of logic. Without judging your feelings, put them to one side while you look at your options from a factual, or intellectual perspective. This may be difficult to do—so difficult, in fact, that some people breeze past this step, saying to themselves, "Yeah, I know all that's true, but how I feel is more important." A lot of impulsive decisions are made that way.

Shopping is a time when we're really tested. Our responsible, budget-minded side has to fight off dual pressures: the salesperson who says, "You deserve it," and our piggy part that wants *everything!*

When she was trying to decide whether or not to keep her baby, Melinda's logical side let her down a bit. For example, she assumed that her child would feel rejected if she gave it up for adoption. Talking to adopted children and adults would have helped her discover if that belief, or assumption, was true. Although it would have taken considerable courage, she might have asked another question. Would they have preferred to have been raised by a young and unwed biological mother, or by their adopted parents?

Step 5: Establish Priorities.

How do your various options fit in with your priorities? If you're saving money to buy a car, buying a new stereo system now might not be your first priority. Or, if the sound system turns into something you don't want to do without, you might ask yourself whether you want to set aside your long-term goal of buying a car.

Step 6: Make Your Decision and "Go for It."

Once you've gone through all five steps thoroughly, you've probably reached a good decision. Now it's important to set aside any lingering doubts and put your energy into carrying out your decision. A positive, hopeful attitude can strongly influence how well things turn out. It's kind of like studying and grades. If you study like mad for a biology test your chance of getting a good grade is excellent. If you wishy-wash around, get distracted, and glance at your book an hour before the test, you probably won't do as well. It's the same with decisions. You've got to go for it.

Chapter Eight

How to Be Assertive

When you reach your teens, the balance of power between you and your parents shifts. Granted, they're still in charge, and it is "their house," but now you possess the verbal and intellectual skills you need to express your thoughts and feelings. But some teenagers still feel powerless when they deal with their parents and rely on leftover childlike ways to get their points across. Amy, who doesn't like her curfew, grumbles about being treated like a five-year-old, and gets even with her parents by coming in late. If John's parents remind him that the garbage needs emptying, he snaps, "I know, I know, I'll do it during the commercial!" Then he forgets.

Amy and John (perhaps like you) haven't had the opportunity, yet, to learn how to deal with their parents assertively. Assertiveness, by the way, means saying what you feel, think, want or don't want, without putting the other person down. It also takes into consideration other people's needs, which usually involves compromise.

It falls mid-way between passive behavior (saying what you want indirectly) and aggressiveness (demanding what you want without concern for anyone else's feelings). Assertiveness is easy to learn, but it can feel strange and kind of nervy at first.

Step 1: Discover What You Feel

Before you try telling someone else what you want, you'll want to check in with yourself and see what you're feeling. When Amy consulted her feelings, she found she hated her curfew not only because it was too early, but also because she felt like a baby having to get in so much earlier than the other kids in her group.

A hint about feelings: often surface feelings like anger, coldness, and indifference cover up our softer, more vulnerable feelings, such as hurt, jealousy, and disappointment. We get mad at a person when we feel they've hurt us or let us down.

So, when you inventory your feelings and come up with "pissed," dig a little deeper and see what's underneath. Once you know this deeper feeling, that's the one to share. It's more honest to say "My feelings are hurt" than to say "You really piss me off." It's also easier for other people: rather than feeling attacked and then getting ready to attack you back, they can pay attention to what you really want to talk about—your feelings.

Rob, a heavily muscled varsity wrestler, came to therapy feeling frustrated by his perfectionistic father, Keith. He was so angry at his father he was afraid he was going to deck him. Rob had brought home his excellent report card; Keith had ignored the A's and demanded to know why he got a couple of B's. Although Rob was used to this drill, he still felt unappreciated. On the surface, he showed rage and dejection: "What's the use? I can never please the jerk."

Rob and I discussed his problem, and after he unloaded some of his rage, his hurt and discouraged feelings surfaced. With encouragement he decided to discuss his feelings with his dad. Rob heartily agreed that his quick-tempered father was apt to be far more receptive if Rob focused on his hurt, rather than his anger.

Step 2: Assess Your Chances

Any time you have to talk over a touchy subject or problem with another person, it's useful to first do some preliminary assessment. Is it likely that talking over the situation will change things or should you save your breath? If your mother, for instance, has said ten times that you cannot have a dog, does it make sense to discuss it one more time? Probably not. But you may have an excellent chance of reaching a compromise on another issue. It makes good sense to pick your battles rather carefully.

Step 3: Choose Good Timing

Think about your timing. Don't try to talk over a problem while you're angry, when time is short, or when a bunch of people are around. With a parent, don't bring up a problem the minute he or she drags in from work. Wait until people have relaxed and had something to eat. Almost all of us are at our worst right before dinner: our blood sugar levels have dropped, causing us to feel tense and irritable. Therapists call this time the "arsenic hour."

Another deadly time to try to discuss a problem or feeling with a parent is while he or she is at work. Most parents hate discussions then because they're in a terrible bind. They can't talk freely or comfortably. Nor do they really have the time to go into your problem in depth, so they feel under the gun to give you a quick answer.

On the other hand, don't be put off by, "Not now, I'm too busy," or tired, or whatever. Ask what would be a better time and make a firm appointment. "Okay, then we'll talk after the football game, right?" Another good time to discuss problems or feelings is after a meal, when people can focus on the conversation and not be distracted by other tasks. Since people are pretty relaxed on the weekends, that is also a good time to talk.

Step 4: Describe What Happens

Begin by describing, as precisely as you can, what happens that you don't like. Stay away from your feelings at this point and stick to the facts. It's like giving the other person an "instant replay" of the problem. Rob said to his father, "When I show you my report card, you notice my B's, but ignore my A's." This pared-down description left out feelings entirely. Rob also avoided loaded words such as "always" and "never," which probably would have made his father defensive. Another drawback to using those words is that the other person can usually find one exception to "never" or "always." Your point is lost.

After you describe the specific facts, pause and give your listener time to recall the scene. Be prepared: this person may not remember what you're talking about, or may recall the incident differently. He or she may even blow up and insist that it didn't happen like that at all. At this point, it's tempting to get into a contest about whose facts are correct. A way around that is to "agree to disagree." You could say, "Okay, you remember it one way and I remember it another."

If your listener still wants to fight about the facts and can't seem to move on, then you should probably end the discussion. Let him or her calm down and bring up the issue at another time.

Step 5: Say How You Feel

Now add your feelings to the discussion of what's bothering you. "When you just notice my B's I feel really wiped out, you know, hurt. Like I can never please you. Then I get discouraged and figure, why should I even try?" Contrast this with what Rob might say if he were angry: "All you do is criticize, criticize, criticize. Nothing ever pleases you."

Step 6: Ask for a Specific Change

After you've discussed what you don't like, describe how you would like things to be. Rob said to his father, "Do you think next time I bring home my report card you could talk about the good stuff first? Then, if you just gotta mention my B's, you could do that after."

Sometimes the change you're asking for may involve your doing something different, too. Let's say it's your job to wash the dishes, and you destest it. Tell your parents that you're sick of doing the dishes and then *offer a deal*. "If you'll do the dishes, I'll clean the bathrooms—both of them." In other words, if they'll change some part of their behavior, you will, too.

Step 7: The Other Person's Side

Once you've expressed your feelings and asked for a specific change, find out how the other person feels. You can do this by simply asking, "What do you think?" or "How does this sound to you?" Rob might ask, "Are you willing to do that, Dad?" or "Is this okay with you?" If you get agreement, or acknowledgment of your feelings, be sure to say thanks!

What do you do if the other person doesn't want to change his behavior or compromise with you? Take a deep breath and try to stay calm, even if you're angry. When you are fairly controlled, tell the other person how you feel: frustrated, hurt, let down, angry, or any combination of those feelings.

Take some time to think over the situation. You may decide that it's hopeless and drop it. Another alternative is to wait and bring it up again. Perhaps the other person will be more receptive the next time.

How to Relax

Your body responds to dramatic or upsetting events by kicking in a chemical called adrenaline. Adrenaline mobilizes you, gets you ready for action. If you're enraged at someone, for instance, the adrenaline says, "Never mind being civilized, punch 'em out." Or, during finals week, it senses your fear and tension and says, "Run! Get out of here!"

At other times your feelings are less intense; you just feel restless and uneasy and have that "ants-in-your-pants" feeling. When you know how to relax, you increase your options: you can stay calm and in control and not feel you have to *do* something when you have a strong feeling. You can think things through.

When you know how to relax yourself, you can do it anytime, anywhere, and no one will notice. You may find the following relaxation techniques useful.

Drop Your Jaw!

One of the quickest ways to relax is to open your mouth a little and drop your jaw. That's what your mouth and jaw do when you're asleep and the most relaxed. It works when you're awake, too.

Deep Breathing

When we get nervous we breathe quickly and only use the top part of our lungs. This makes us short of breath and even more nervous. Deep breathing can prevent that from happening.

You can deep breathe while you're standing, sitting, or lying down. While you're learning it, it's fun to do it lying down. Put a towel or mat on the floor and lie down in a "dead-body" pose. Extend your legs and flop them apart with your toes pointing outward. Put your arms at your side, not touching your body. Turn the palms of your hands up, and close your eyes.

First, scan your body for tension. Start with your toes and notice if there's any tension in them. Slowly move your attention up your entire body to the top of your head, taking note of any place you feel tense. Don't try to do anything about the tension. Just notice it.

Before you begin the breathing exercise, bring your legs up and bend your knees, leaving your feet about eight inches apart. Make sure your spine is straight. Now, inhale deeply through your *nose*, keeping your mouth closed. Hold your breath for three seconds. It takes three seconds to say, "One thousand one, one thousand two, one thousand three." Exhale your breath through your *mouth*. Relax your mouth, tongue, and jaw.

Continue deep breathing for ten minutes. Practice this each day for about two weeks. You'll find that the process becomes automatic. Try it (sitting up) at school, or while you're watching TV. Look around to see if anyone is noticing what you're doing. It's doubtful they will because this is a very subtle way to relax.

Deep Muscle Relaxation

This exercise is similar to deep breathing. You'll probably want to learn it in privacy, but then you can do it on the sly any time you feel tense. If you have any injuries, wait until they're healed. If you should feel pain at any time, discontinue the exercises.

Lie down in the dead-body position and scan your body for tension. With your eyes closed imagine the most relaxing place on earth. For some it's the beach, for others the mountains. Some people picture themselves lying in front of the fireplace. Pick your own relaxing place and picture yourself in it. Imagine sounds you might hear, the way things feel, fragrances in the air. This relaxing location is called your "safe place."

Next, tighten and relax all the major muscle groups in your body. This is how you do it:

1. Point your toes away from your face and hold them there for the count of three. Relax and now point your toes toward your head and hold them for three more seconds. Relax your feet completely and let them return to a comfortable position.

2. Tighten your calf muscles, hold for three seconds and relax. Take a deep breath between exercising each muscle group.

3. Now, tighten your thigh muscles. You can do that by putting your knees together. Each time you tighten one muscle group, try to keep other muscles relaxed.

4. Next tighten your buttocks and then relax. Now suck in your stomach and hold it three seconds. Relax.

5. Tighten and release the muscles in your hands by squeezing them into tight balls. Hold three seconds and relax. Do the same thing with your forearms and biceps.

6. To relax your shoulders, first pull them toward the center of your body and hold. Then relax and pull them back as if they could touch in the middle of your back. Relax.

7. Tension loves to settle in your neck, so you may find it stiff. Begin by trying to bring your right ear drum to your right shoulder. Return your head upright and then do the same thing with your left ear. Relax. Now, bring your chin forward, as if you were going to touch it to your chest. Gently push your head back. Hold and relax.

8. Tightening your facial muscles is fun. Scrunch up the muscles in your face to the ugliest look you can imagine. Bare your teeth, tighten your jaw, lift your eyebrows. Hold and then relax.

9. Now scan your body once more. Are you still tense anywhere? If so, tighten those muscles again and then relax. That should take away the tension.

After you've practiced this exercise for several weeks, you'll notice that the minute you begin (with your feet), your whole body will relax. It's almost as if your first "tightening" cues the rest of your body to relax. That's why you can do this in public and no one will know. Start with your feet and perhaps go up through your legs, and first thing you know you'll be considerably more relaxed. Or you can start with your hands and move up your arms. Again, no one will notice.

Since you practice this exercise by going to your "safe place" first, you'll find that sometimes you can just do that, and you'll relax automatically.

Chapter Ten

Handling a Crisis

Handling a crisis is scary for teenagers. Often it's the first time in their lives they've had to deal with a serious problem. Many things make a crisis seem overwhelming. Not only is the problem serious, but it's usually unexpected.

All of a sudden you find yourself in a mess and don't know how to fix it. Crises are generally serious enough that you end up telling your parents. That sounds dreadful, too. It's easy to picture them yelling at you, throwing you out, and staying mad forever. But parents rarely act like that. They may get upset at first. Then they calm down and try to help.

They don't flip out because they've been through their own crises and have learned how to cope. They also have a different view of what's serious and what isn't. The first week Tim had his driver's license, he crashed into a parked car. He called his mother at work and told her in a trembling voice what he'd done. His mother was upset, but as she put it, "It ruined my day, but not my life."

For a while, Tim was so scared that he couldn't think straight. He was sure he'd never be able to drive again, that his stepfather would never forgive him, and that he'd lose his driver's license. After he talked to his parents that night, he calmed down and began to put his accident in perspective. Even his punishment—not being able to drive alone for a month—seemed bearable.

Tim was especially dreading his stepfather's reaction. But instead of being mad, his stepfather was helpful. He told Tim how to file an accident report and how to get the damaged car home. So, when you've got a problem, consider letting your parents help. They won't think less of you; they've made mistakes themselves. That's why they can be understanding.

If your parents aren't together enough to be helpful, consider turning to some other calm and capable adult. You'll find it comforting having someone mature and stable to lean on.

Grades and College

If you've received a disappointing grade, you're probably discouraged and down on yourself. Before you share your news, try to get some perspective on what that grade means. First, is it a midterm grade that you can raise by the end of the semester? In most cases, it is semester grades that will go on your transcript, not your midterm grades.

Next, realistically assess the damage. Are your grades really low, like D's and F's, or are they just not as good as you wanted? If you are college-bound and crushed because you got a 'B' or 'C', that is no reason to self-destruct. You may need to change your strategy a little. If your grade point average (GPA) is in jeopardy, consider going to summer school so you can add another 'A' or 'B' to your transcript. You can also pull up your GPA by doing better next semester.

Third, keep in mind that your SAT scores, school activities, and entrance essay also weigh heavily in acceptance to college. You may be strong enough in these areas to get into the college you want.

If you know for sure that this particular low grade will

keep you out of your first-choice college, here are two tips to help you with your disappointment: Let yourself feel your sadness. Mourn, cry, and droop around for a day or two. But do not despair or tell yourself it's the end of your world. This is a setback but not a catastrophe.

Then, after you've given yourself time to absorb your disappointment, consider other colleges. At first, none of them may look as good as your first choice, but give it time. Other schools will start looking better.

The fourth part of putting things in perspective is to consider whom you're trying to please with your grades. Is it yourself, your friends, or your parents? Or is it all three? If you're working your rear end off to please someone else, it's much harder to stay motivated and to succeed. Use this setback to figure out what *you* want. If you don't know, take the time to think it through. Most teens take about six years to settle on a career choice.

When you've digested your disappointment and figured out what your grades mean to you, then tell your parents. If they have a fit, you'll be prepared to take it if you have thought the whole thing through ahead of time. Share those thoughts with your parents. That way, they'll know you're also concerned.

Consistently Low Grades

If your report card is loaded with D's and F's, something other than school is probably wrong in your life. You may feel your grades are low because you don't like school or because you're bored. But getting consistently low marks is a sign that something else is awry. Try not to con yourself by thinking you'll do better next semester. If you can do better, great. Usually, it's more realistic to look at your low grades as a warning light, signaling that something is bothering you. Spend the next few weeks figuring out what that is. If you aren't able to do that, ask for help. Talking to a counselor might help you find out what is troubling you and help you figure out how to improve your life.

Pregnancy

Facing an unplanned pregnancy can be crushing. At first, you may feel as if you were in shock: "This can't be real; this can't be happening to me." Then you have to decide what to do, which is what this section explores. Because the choices are different for young women than for young men, the issues are discussed separately.

If You Are Pregnant

You've missed one or two periods and you think you may be pregnant. What should you do? First, find out for sure if you are. There are many public health clinics, Planned Parenthood offices, and private physicians that you can go to for a test that will give you the results in just a few minutes.

In most states your visit to a clinic or Planned Parenthood will be confidential. This means no one can tell your parents anything, or even that you've had an appointment. Since there are a few states that do not protect teenagers' confidentiality, you might want to ask about this before you go in.

You also have the option of using one of the early pregnancy test kits available at drug stores. These are fairly expensive, $12 to $18, but if you follow the instructions carefully, they can be quite accurate.

Once you've determined that you're pregnant, tell the baby's father. Not only is he entitled to know, but you can use his support and consider his ideas and feelings while you figure out what to do.

The next decision is a hard one. Should you tell your parents? In most cases, I think the answer is yes. Even though they will be upset, and perhaps angry, they love you and will want to help. They can probably also give you excellent advice and support. If you decide to have your baby, they will have to know anyway. If you decide to have an abortion, they can help you through that experience, too.

When shouldn't you tell your parents? I would not tell them if doing so would put you, or the baby's father, in any kind of physical danger. It might also be hard to tell them if they are likely to overreact, for instance, by restricting you to your home for many weeks or abusing you emotionally by calling you names, lecturing you, and chastising you for days or months on end.

If you don't tell your parents, it would be wise to discuss your situation with an adult you trust—a friend's parent, a teacher, a relative, a counselor or a religious counselor. Your decision is such a huge one that you might benefit from the experience and perspective of an older person.

The next decision is the big one: what to do about your pregnancy. Discuss this long and hard with the baby's father. This decision will affect his whole life, just as it will yours, and both of you should be involved in it. Listen carefully to his feelings. They are just as important as yours. If you can't agree, ask an adult to help the two of you discuss it. A counselor from Planned Parenthood might be helpful. Planned Parenthood is "pro choice," which means they won't be pushing you one way or the other. They're just interested in helping you make a decision that will work for you. With the help of an objective third party, you may be able to reach a decision with which you both can live. Unfortunately, this was not the case with Dawn and Jose.

A few weeks after Jose and Dawn broke up, Dawn discovered she was pregnant. She secretly hoped her pregnancy would get them back together, but it didn't. Jose was kind, but adamant that she should have an abortion. Out of hurt, anger, and revenge, Dawn decided to "fix" Jose and have the baby. The baby is three now and although Dawn accepts Jose's financial support, she continues to get even with him by refusing to let him see his daughter. She rationalizes her selfish and immature behavior by saying that it's what Jose deserves since he didn't want the baby in the first place.

This couple could not agree on what to do, and they all pay a terrible price. The following are issues to think about as you wrestle with your decision:

The baby. Can you offer it a normal, secure, and loving life? Are you and the baby's father mature enough to be good parents? Do you earn enough money to raise a child? Who will care for the baby if you work? In what ways will the baby be affected by having either an unwed mother or very young parents?

You. Do you want a baby at this time in your life? Have you completed your educational or occupational goals? Are you able to support yourself in such a way that your life will still be fun and interesting if you have to support a child, too? Are you willing or able to sacrifice your time to raise a child? Will you shortchange your future life by having a baby now?

Your values. How do your choices fit with your values? Will you feel *relatively* at peace with your choice?

I stress the word relatively because you can reasonably expect to feel some degree of guilt. You're not an awful person who's done an unforgivable thing, but your decision involves life or the potential for life, depending on how you see it. Almost everyone in this situation feels some degree of guilt. But that doesn't mean your decision is wrong. It just means you're in a dilemma. Don't let guilt consume you or cause you to hate yourself.

If Your Girlfriend Is Pregnant

If your girlfriend is pregnant, the issues you face are somewhat the same as hers: telling your parents, going through the agony of figuring out what to do, and dealing with guilt. You may also encounter another difficulty. Your girlfriend carries the baby during pregnancy, and so she has the final say about what happens; you may or may not like her decision. Since it will affect you the rest of your life, it's important that you be as active as you can in making the decision with her. Don't assume the problem and decision are out of your hands, so you can just fade away. If you do, everyone loses.

Insist on being included. Even if you and your baby's mother disagree about what to do, she will not feel so alone making this important decision. And you'll know you have done all you can. If necessary, ask a mature third party to help the two of you talk over your decision.

If you have talked all you can and you're not happy with the outcome, you have a tough job ahead of you. It's in your best interest somehow to accept your girlfriend's decision— not because she knows what's best and not because it's fair, but because the law gives her the final say.

Help yourself by talking about your frustration and helplessness. That, and time, will help you come to terms with it. You may take months to adjust to the outcome of this problem. Be patient. If guilt gets you down, take another look at what you expect of yourself. You have done the best you can under rough circumstances.

Tickets and Accidents

Getting your first ticket can be upsetting and embarrassing. To put it in perspective, though, try looking at the episode as a mistake or an error in judgment, which is normal. Use the experience to help you be a more conscientious driver and don't be hard on yourself.

If you've gotten several tickets, however, you're not taking good care of yourself or your passengers. It's tempting to rationalize your tickets by thinking that you've just been especially unlucky. But that's not the point. You need to look at why you're putting yourself at risk so often. What is it about you, or your life, that allows you to play so free and easy with your survival? Are you angry about something? Is anything else getting you down?

Begin looking at your unhappy feelings, the things that are bugging you, and make an effort not to act them out when you drive. (Also see Chapter 4.) It's tempting to floor the gas pedal when you're angry and to take risks when you don't like yourself, but there are many safer ways to express your feelings. You might find the chapters on assertiveness and self-esteem helpful.

Trouble with the Law

Few things are more shattering than finding yourself in trouble with the law. Whether you've been hauled in for drunk driving or been caught shoplifting, the experience is traumatic.

If this has happened to you, don't let screwy thinking (see Chapter 5) turn this experience into a catastrophe. Many teenagers who get into jams think about suicide. Embarrassed, humiliated, or full of self-hate, they feel overwhelmed by the idea of facing family, friends, and consequences. They are in pain and despair, longing for a way out.

If you have these feelings, don't act on them. Things are not hopeless. They are painful and scary right now, but they will get better, even though you can't see how. Don't try to look ahead too far. People do not think well in the middle of a crisis. Focus on how you can get through each hour.

Later, when you're calmer, you can assess your situation. First, let's look at your crime. Unless you're innocent, you've broken a law—a law you probably knew about. Sometimes we risk doing something illegal because we think we can get away with it. We know it's possible to get caught, but we think it's unlikely. That's what happened to Eric.

Seventeen-year-old Eric's parents got a call at three o'clock one morning from the police. They said Eric had been arrested for possession of alcohol. He'd approached an older guy going into the liquor store and asked him to buy him a six-pack. The guy said yes, and Eric gave him the money. When the guy came out of the store, he handed Eric the beer. Two minutes later, police surrounded Eric's car. Although obtaining liquor this way is common in Eric's town, he just happened to get caught.

If this is the kind of thing you've done, it isn't inhuman or awful. You took a risk, and it didn't pay off. Taking risks and dealing with the consequences is part of adolescence. It is serious, but it can also be valuable. Next time you're considering breaking a law you may decide it just isn't worth the consequences.

Teenagers sometimes commit crimes when they're with a bunch of other kids who are egging them on, or with a group that is drinking. If those were your circumstances, you have learned something important about yourself: being in a group that's getting rowdy can affect your judgment. If the group looks like it's headed for trouble, either by drinking too much or getting into mischief, you can protect yourself by leaving. Momentary approval or disapproval from your friends is just that—momentary.

What if you have no idea why you've done something like shoplifting, for instance, or something else impulsive and unplanned? Chapter 4 can help you discover whether you were acting out feelings you didn't even know you had. See if you can figure out what those feelings are and begin talking them over with someone. That will go a long way toward helping you solve the underlying problem that got you in trouble in the first place. If you don't know what's bothering you and don't know why you've broken the law, then it's time to get counseling. That's what counselors do—help you know and understand yourself better.

Most teens who break laws spend some time in Juvenile Hall. Whether it's for a day or months, they dread the idea of going there. If you're terrified, as most kids are, do what you can to get ready for the experience. First, find out everything you can about it. Drive by and look the hall over carefully. Notice if there are outdoor facilities where the kids are doing physical ed. What are they wearing? How do they look? Do their faces look miserable or are some of them laughing?

Then ask the juvenile officer assigned to you what the daily schedule is like. Will you have free time? If so, what can you do with it? Are there televisions? How many visitors can you have? What are the hours? Before you go, find out about public transportation, so your friends can come see you. They will help a lot.

A fifteen-year-old male client of mine who thought he might have to go to Juvenile Hall said flat out that he'd run away first. When I asked why, he hemmed and hawed and finally mumbled something about getting raped. He'd heard that this happened all the time. I told him I had not heard that, but if it was true he could protect himself by putting himself on suicide watch. This means someone on staff comes by every five minutes or so to check on kids who are in danger of killing themselves. While asking for a suicide watch might be manipulative, it would protect him from rape.

If you are fortunate enough to avoid going to Juvenile Hall or jail, you'll still want to do some emotional work with yourself to keep your law-breaking in perspective. This was true for Pete, who lived in a small farming community, where his father was the mayor of the town and his mother a librarian. One hot, boring summer, he and his younger brother, Brad, went on crime forays. Neither Pete, who had just turned thirteen, nor his younger brother, who was eleven, thought of their behavior as criminal. It felt more like a teenage version of cops and robbers. They did things like breaking into the corner market late at night to steal candy bars and snooping around in the homes of neighbors away on vacation.

Eventually the boys were caught. Both vividly remember being towed around town by the local police, returning to their various crime scenes. Of course, a lot of people saw them in the police car, and those who didn't heard about it anyway. The brothers were mortified, but their story gets worse. A few months later their father lost his bid for reelection. In disgrace, the family moved to another town.

This was not a family that talked openly about things, so the boys mistakenly concluded that their father had lost the election because of what they had done. Guilt-ridden and shamed, they spent many years trying to be perfect to make up for the heartbreak they believed they had caused their family. Only when they were in their thirties did these two brothers learn that their father had lost the election because of politics, not because of their behavior.

So be very careful not to overdramatize the effect that your crime has on your family. While your family no doubt hurts for you and worries about the pain you're experiencing, no one is going to jump off the nearest bridge because you screwed up. You shouldn't either.

Physical and Sexual Abuse

Being sexually molested and being beaten up are very different horrible experiences. Yet they have certain traits in common.

Con Jobs

Both kinds of abuse involve con jobs. Young people who are sexually abused are frequently told it's happening "for their own good." A stepfather, for instance, may tell his stepdaughter that he wants to "prepare" her for sex, to show her how it's done so boys won't just take advantage of her. After all, she's very pretty and boys are going to chase after her. Besides, her mother is so cold sexually that he, the molester, has to have an outlet. Of course, these are not legitimate reasons; they are sick rationalizations. The stepfather does not have his stepdaughter's best interest in mind, at all. He's just selling her a bill of goods to keep her quiet.

Victims of physical abuse get the same kind of manipulative message: that they are in some way to blame. Either their behavior is so rotten that their abuser has no choice, or they're being beaten because their abuser has to "teach them a lesson." In other words, the victims are abused because they are either so bad or so beautiful. Never does the abuser own up to the fact that he or she is completely out of control. According to the abuser, it's the kid's fault.

Intimidation and Threats

Kids who are abused are frightened into not telling. Sexual abusers often claim that their victims will be responsible for breaking up the parents' marriage, as well as the family, if they tell anyone. Or they say no one will believe the kid's story. Abusers also say they'll be arrested and carted off to jail if their victims tell the police. Sometimes molesters ensure silence by threatening to molest younger kids in the family.

Physically abused teens are easy to frighten into silence, too. They hear things like, "I'll kill you if you tell," or "If you think this is bad, wait and see what happens if anyone finds out. Then you'll really hurt." These threats are blackmail, and all too often they work. Victims are terrified and don't know where to turn.

Shame

Even if they aren't blackmailed into silence, some teens feel too ashamed to tell anyone about their abuse. They buy the story that they're to blame and feel that they're the only person this is happening to. They feel alone in their nightmare. One young woman put it this way: "I couldn't talk about it. I couldn't even bring myself to use the right words when I thought about it. But if I had been walking down the street and there was a sign that said, 'If bad things are happening to you at home, come in here,' I would have walked right in and told. But that's not how it is."

It Feels a Little Bit Good

Young people are further confused and shamed by the fact that sometimes some parts of sexual molestation briefly feel good. That is very normal. It doesn't mean the victims are bad, nor does it change the fact that these sexual acts were forced on them.

Gary, for instance, was molested by his uncle from the time he was sixteen until he was twenty. He hated it, yet now and then he was aroused and got an erection. He felt guilty, as though that in some way made him a willing participant.

Coping

Teenagers respond to their physical or sexual abuse in many different ways. Some get through the horror by learning not to feel. They shut off, go blank, become someone else while it's going on. A social worker told the following story:

One time she was driving a girl from the children's center to her foster home. They had driven a few blocks when the social worker noticed that the girl had a funny look on her face. She asked what was wrong, and the girl very calmly said, "My finger's caught in the door." The social worker pulled over to the side of the road, dashed around to the girl's side of the car, and gingerly opened the door. Her index finger was stuck in there, smashed. The girl did not feel the pain because she had trained herself to stop feeling while she was being beaten.

When abused teens feel dead inside, they occasionally do bizarre and dreadful things to feel alive again. They slash themselves with knives or mutilate themselves in other ways. Sexually abused girls often become promiscuous, anorexic, or bulimic. And, of course, abused teens of both sexes run away from home. They also become depressed: they have layers and layers of rage and pain that they can't express to *anyone*. In time that anger becomes directed against themselves, and they grow depressed and suicidal.

What to Do

If you are abused, you must get help. Getting help means telling someone, and that may be very, very hard for you. You love your family and perhaps even the person abusing you. The idea of telling anyone about him or her sounds terrible. But by telling, you make it possible to get help not only for yourself, but for everyone in your family—especially the person who abuses you. That person is sick and needs help but does not know how to ask for it. Many abusive parents have said they were relieved when their kids told and the whole thing was out in the open. Although they felt guilty about what they were doing, they couldn't stop by themselves. It's also hard to tell because your abuser has brainwashed you into believing that telling will lead to dire consequences. The next section explains what really happens (in most cases) when you tell.

Whom to Tell

You can choose from among a whole range of adults who will get you help. In most states, the law requires doctors, nurses, counselors, and teachers to make a report when they suspect a young person is being abused. They report this information either to a government agency, such as Child Protective Services, or to the police. You can also go to the police directly and tell them yourself. Be assured that whomever you choose to tell will not blame you.

What Happens When You Tell

If you report being physically abused, the police will go to your home and most likely arrest the person who is abusing you. While this sounds terrible, remember it is the first step in getting help for your family.

If you report sexual abuse, your molester will probably be arrested. The authorities may take you to the safety of a relative's home or to a children's center; it's also possible that you'll be allowed to remain in your own home. Either way, the goal is to end your abuse.

Another possibility is that many days may pass before anything happens. It may be that someone from Child Protective Services will merely contact your family and begin an investigation. How fast things happen depends mostly on how much danger the authorities think you are in.

Questions

At some point someone will question you about the abuse. This may be hard for you to talk about. That's very common, and it may take several visits with the investigator before you can discuss it. In the meantime, though, be sure to nod your head "yes" when you're asked whether you have been abused.

Boys who have been sexually abused by a male often have an especially hard time talking about what happened because they're afraid that other people may think they are gay. Adults understand that this isn't so. Being molested by a male doesn't mean the victim is gay or will ever become gay.

The investigator's visits are good times to ask any questions you might have. You'll undoubtedly be worried about what's going to happen over the next few months, and the investigator can tell you as much as he or she knows. It's possible the person who abused you will spend some time in jail. It may be that the courts will make the abuser live away from home for a while and order your entire family to have counseling.

No matter what the outcome, remember you are not responsible. You did not cause the problem in the first place. You only loved yourself and your family enough to get help.

Being Dumped By Your Boyfriend or Girlfriend

When the person you love wants to end your relationship, it hurts like hell. It feels like a death, as though part of you is dying, or someone you loved has died. In some ways it's even worse than that: the person you love is still around; he or she just doesn't want to see you anymore. Can anything be more painful?

People respond to rejection differently. Some become stiff-spined and try to banish the other person from their thoughts. They don't want to see the person, talk about him or her, or remember any part of the relationship. They internalize their pain, which means keeping it inside. Others externalize it: they talk about their feelings to get it out in the open, and they feel better. They need to rehash what happened, speculate about what caused it, and ask "Why?" a few hundred times. Which type are you?

Neither way is better. They are just different ways people cope with their losses. Eventually both types may need to get what is called closure on their relationship before they can accept it ending. Let's say, for instance, that your girlfriend has told you that she doesn't want to see you anymore. She says it's not because anything is wrong with you; it's just that she doesn't want to be tied down to one person. She doesn't think that's healthy. While she's telling you this, it makes sense. Actually you're so stunned you really can't take in what she's saying.

Later, you think over the things she's said and want to know more. Did you do something wrong? When did she start feeling this way? Why did she change? Is there someone else? Each person has different questions. If you want to know these things, ask. You're entitled to know. The answers may help you understand her reasoning. That will make it easier for you to accept her decision, to come to closure. Don't let pride prevent you from asking. You have nothing to lose. She's already said it's over. Another advantage of talking over why is that you can learn things about yourself. It helped Jake.

Practically every girl in the junior class agrees that Jake is a hunk. He's not only good looking, but he's a star athlete and has a reputation for being a good lover. The problem is he can't keep a girlfriend. When his first two girlfriends dropped him, he was hurt but he didn't let it get to him. There were lots of other girls available.

When the third girl, Wendy, dumped him, he was upset enough to talk it over with her. He discovered that Wendy couldn't stand his arrogance, his "Mr. Cool" attitude. As they talked he could see how offensive that behavior was, and he realized it was really a big cover-up. Inside, Jake's not at all sure of himself. He acts like Mr. Cool, so no one will know how insecure he often feels.

Once you understand what went wrong in your relationship, the tough work begins—mourning. This means letting yourself feel hurt, lost and lonely. How long this miserable period lasts depends upon a couple of factors. One is how intense and deep your relationship was. The other is how long it lasted. If you were very close for many months or more, you may feel blue for at least a month. If your relationship was less intense, you may bounce back sooner. Either way, the pain will end. It does take time, though, and there don't seem to be any shortcuts.

In the meantime you can do certain things to feel better. After you've allowed yourself an "official moaning around time," don't wallow in memories. When thoughts of him or her float up, do your best to dash them from your mind. Think of the present or future rather than the past. Pick out new music rather than listening to "your song," or other music from the time you were together. If you have love letters or notes, burn 'em. Some people have great fun getting rid of all the stuff that has to do with him or her. You may get satisfaction from flushing flushable things down the toilet (there's a nice symbolism there). Haul other memorabilia to the trashcan and throw it in with all your might. That feels good, too.

These actions allow you to rid yourself of your anger in a safe and gratifying way. Feeling angry if you've been rejected goes with the territory. In fact, if you don't let yourself experience your anger and get it out by talking about it, or physically expressing it in a safe way, you run the risk of turning that anger toward yourself, with or without meaning to, and getting depressed. When you've gone through your mourning and anger, move on. You may want to be solo for a while, or find a new relationship.

Chapter Eleven

Family Problems

Vicki comes from a close-knit Italian family. Her father is rather old-fashioned and has firm beliefs about duty and loyalty. He and Vicki fight over a bunch of issues, but one guarantees fireworks—family gatherings. Vicki thinks they're boring, but her father insists she attend each one. He wants her to experience the closeness and continuity that comes from family. She couldn't care less. Neither of them is willing to compromise.

Their problems, perhaps like those you have with your parents, are not just Vicki's fault or her Dad's fault. Both people are responsible for their conflicts. Each could change the outcome of their argument by changing his or her attitude or behavior. So far, both have been unwilling to change, partly because the issue is larger than family gatherings. The underlying issue is who's in charge of Vicki.

Vicki further inflames her father by the way she argues. Sarcastic and critical to him, she bursts into tears if he criticizes her. Actually, Vicki's contradictory behavior is normal for teenagers.

Sensitivity

If your feelings bruise easily, you might find it helpful to understand why. Right now your self-esteem is as stable as a heap of jello: the slightest bump and the whole thing starts wiggling and shaking. In a flash, you can go from feeling okay about yourself to hating everything about your life. That's because you're in no-man's-land. A few years ago you could do nothing wrong. Your parents adored you, and you basked in their love. Then you got older and your parents started *expecting* things of you. If you didn't comply, they looked at you through narrowed eyes and asked, "Why not?" Sometimes they got mad or critical, and that put the first dent in your self-confidence.

About the same time, you started comparing yourself to other kids and found you had all sorts of horrible imperfections. Your self-esteem plummeted further. So now you've arrived at the age of self-loathing. The last thing you can handle is more criticism. You therefore deflect your parents' attacks with a stink that would make a skunk envious. You lash back by hollering, by saying something that will cut them to the quick, or by going on the attack.

Criticism

Ironically, while you're easily hurt by criticism, you can be critical of everyone else—especially your parents. They get it for several reasons. First, you're supposed to leave the nest in a few years. That's a tad scary, but less so if the nest's a mess. So you start picking at it—finding fault with everything from the furniture to your mother's hairstyle.

Second, people who feel lousy about themselves often put other people down to give themselves a boost. You may be a wreck, but if your parents are a disaster, you can feel better about yourself for a few minutes. This strategy doesn't have staying power, though. You soon feel awful because you know you've been mean.

You may also criticize your parents because, God forbid, people might think you're like them! That is what Zack thought.

Zack worried about what other kids thought about his mother. She was sort of a leftover hippie with limp, grey-streaked hair hanging straight down around her face. Her clothes were mismatched and droopy, her legs unshaven. When she dropped Zack off at school in her aging VW van, he used to duck down so no one would see him.

When I saw him in therapy, Zack was trying to make new friends and especially wanted to be accepted by this one group of guys. They had "normal looking" parents who drove BMWs. He was convinced his friends wouldn't have a thing to do with him if they got a look at his mother. Enraged at her appearance, he'd pick fights with her about other issues.

Zack and I discussed whether his feelings about other kids were influenced by how their parents looked. He concluded it didn't matter to him at all. In fact, he couldn't even picture the way other parents dressed. That helped him relax about his mother and get off her case.

Moods

Your moodiness may also puzzle your parents. At times you are warm, loving, and appreciative. Other times you are cold and rejecting, and you serve up criticism in elephant-sized spoons. Wary and defensive, your parents aren't sure which you is going to make an appearance. While you can't always control your moodiness, you can get along better with your parents if you'll do two things:

- When you're in a lousy mood, take responsibility for that. Tell them you're acting rotten because you're in a bad mood, not because of anything they've done.
- And, when you know you've been unfair or mean, apologize.

Without meaning to, you may do other things that cause

conflicts with your parents. These behaviors include things that worry them (like not studying, for example) and things that affect them directly (like not doing your chores). Behaviors in the first group affect your independence, and you may prefer not changing them. You may see more sense in changing behaviors that clearly affect your parents.

Below is a partial list of things that drive parents crazy. See if any of these sound familiar. If so, changing one or two of them may make your life smoother at home.

1. Not doing your chores.

2. Not doing your chores thoroughly.

3. Not doing your chores on time.

4. Having to be reminded five times to do your chores.

5. Not keeping your word.

6. Lying.

7. Hogging the phone.

8. Getting phone calls late at night or early in the morning.

9. Borrowing their tools, cosmetics, etc., and misusing them.

10. Borrowing things and not returning them.

11. Loaning your parents' possessions to friends.

12. Taking things without permission.

13. Drinking their booze.

14. Filling up the booze bottle with plain or colored water so they won't know.

15. Pigging down all the Oreos.

16. Eating food your mother planned to fix for dinner.

17. Blocking the driveway with your bike or car.

18. Bringing home their car with an empty gas tank.

19. Slamming doors of any and all kinds.

20. Taking half-hour showers.

21. Turning up the stereo to "deaf."

22. Leaving your stuff lying around the house.

23. Not letting your parents know where you are.

24. Breaking curfew.

25. Using pig-pen table manners.

Your Parents Are Too Strict

Strict parents are frustrating because they restrict your freedom. Their rules also feel like a vote of "no confidence," and that's hard on your self-esteem. You feel like a baby in comparison to your friends. Your parents' tight rules also seem to imply you can't cut it in the adult world.

Getting them to loosen up requires a strategy. Your goal is to get them to relax a rule so they can see how you handle it, kind of like a test case. If you do well, then you can point that out and ask to try it in another area. Start with a small issue first, the one on which you think they would be most willing to give.

Next, think about how to present your idea. Depending on your parents, some approaches will work better than others. Here's one example of how to say it. "Ma, I'd really like to have more freedom, but I know you worry about me. Could we try an experiment? How about if you let me go over to a friends's house after school, instead of coming straight home, for one week? I promise I'll call you the minute I get there and I'll be home by five."

If things go well, ask to try it for two weeks. What you're doing is building your parents' trust in your ability to handle freedom and responsibility. When you use this approach, you're doing several things:

- Acknowledging your parents' feelings and fears.
- Demonstrating that you've thought about these concerns and come up with a plan that takes them into consideration.
- Your plan has specific limits and a trial period so your parents have a chance to see that you can take responsibility.

Here's another approach, but it has to be handled delicately. Sometimes if parents realize other parents are letting their kids do something—go to a beach party, for instance—they feel reassured, especially if they respect the other parents. The trick is making sure you don't get your parents defensive by saying something like, "Well! Mrs. So-and-So is letting John go, what's wrong with you?" Instead, you might try asking your parents to call the So-and-So's to find out why they think it's okay for John to go. This will get your folks talking with other parents, so they'll have an opportunity to compare rules. Your parents may conclude they are being too restrictive.

If none of these ideas work, ask your parents to do some reading about teenagers. Show them this book and ask them to read the parts that you think are important.

Another strategy is to call for reinforcements. Talk to your school counselor, priest, minister, rabbi, or family doctor. Ask him or her to help you talk to your parents. If you strike out there, ask your parents to let you talk to a therapist. As a last resort, see if you can make arrangements to live with another family member—perhaps your grandparent or aunt, someone who is more realistic about teenagers.

Should none of these suggestions work and your parents won't change, you'll probably be quite angry. Find a way to deal with your anger that won't harm you or anyone else. If you're not in danger of getting hit or restricted even further, you might keep telling your parents how frustrated and angry you are with specific rules. Be persistent, like a dripping faucet. This may not change their behavior but the important thing in this situation is to get your anger out in an appropriate and safe manner.

In addition to this, find someone to talk to. Above all, don't keep your feelings bottled up. If you aren't comfortable talking to anyone, then try to drain your anger through physical activity. Run, play ball, chop wood, beat your pillow. Another safe outlet is writing. Many people find it relieving to put their feelings down on paper or to keep a diary. If you decide to keep what you've written, be sure to lock it away in a private place.

Your Parents Reject You

Even more painful than parents who breathe down your neck are parents who just don't seem to care. Unfortunately, there really are parents like this. They range from the overly busy to the extraordinarily destructive.

They're Too Busy

Some parents are too busy and preoccupied with their own careers, interests, and travels to pay much attention to their children. Although they love their kids, they're too immature to put anyone else's needs before their own. They live by the philosophy "me first."

Teenagers commonly react to absentee parents by raising hell. Since the parents are rarely home, their house becomes the local party place. In addition to throwing wild parties, teenagers in these families may drink heavily, do drugs routinely, screw around, or drive recklessly. In short, they rebel in loud and obvious ways to get their parents' attention. Regrettably, it doesn't really work. Preoccupied parents react to their teenagers' escapades with annoyance and anger and rarely look beneath the surface to see that their kids are hurting.

If this description fits your parents, then you've gotten a raw deal. Your parents are not awful people, though; they are selfish people whose behavior has nothing to do with you. Your being perfect would not change them: they wouldn't notice. Or if they did, they'd see your perfection as a reflection of themselves and not give you much credit. So be assured that their selfish nature does not mean anything is lacking in you.

Rather than continuing to "show" your parents how unhappy you are, try to talk to them. Catch them when they are not dashing out the door and ask to talk. Tell them you feel neglected and unimportant. Pull out the calendar and plan some family outings over the next few months. Schedule as many as you can, because it's possible that your parents will let other appointments take priority over family time. See whether you can have one night a week be family night—a time when you at least eat dinner together. If it's too hard to get everyone in the family together at the same time, schedule quality time alone with one parent or the other.

If your parents just don't seem interested, it makes sense for you to give up, at least temporarily. Don't give up on yourself, just on them. Give yourself room to feel your disappointment and talk about it with your friends. Feeling terrifically angry at your parents is normal and appropriate. You don't need to feel guilty or start getting angry at yourself for being mad at them. That's screwy thinking.

Instead of letting your anger consume you, look around for adults who *do* have time for you. What about your grandfather or an uncle? Perhaps you have an adult friend you're close to. Spend time with these people and invest your energy in them. There's no point spinning your wheels trying to get attention from your parents if they are just not going to come through.

They Want You to be Lifeless

A study of suicidal college students revealed that many were the children of parents who didn't want them. As kids they sensed their parents' rejection and did their best to fade into the woodwork. They were quiet children who made no demands on their parents, showed no feelings, and deadened their emotions.

When they left home to go to college, they let themselves feel for the first time in their lives. But this caused them enormous inner conflict. On one hand, they loved the fact that they were feeling, but by doing so they went against their parents' wishes that they be nonexistent. Many tried suicide to achieve the deadness that their parents expected of them.

If you live in this appalling situation, you must have some potent inner strength to have made it this far. Congratulate yourself on your toughness and your ability to survive. You've obviously had to learn to be very adaptable. That's a wonderful trait. Now, to grow and begin living a fuller life, you'll need to discard the emotional deadness your parents expected of you.

I would guess that one reason the college students mentioned earlier became suicidal is that they went from one extreme to another. At home they were expected to be rather ghostlike and fade into the background. At college they were expected to be—and wanted to be—alive, vibrant, excited. That's a huge leap, in a short time, and it can be frightening.

It makes sense to take things more slowly. Begin feeling now, while you're still living at home. You don't need to express your feelings to your parents. Start with your friends: let out your liveliness and vitality with them. Experience how good that feels. At first you may feel twinges of fear, as well. This is normal and usually diminishes quickly. After all, you live in one of the most difficult kinds of families: your parents have brainwashed you into feeling guilty for feeling *anything!*

Slowly expand the situations in which you allow yourself to feel. Perhaps just responding to movies, television shows, and music would be a good start. Then, begin reacting to items in the news that interest you. What you're doing is slowly getting comfortable with feeling so you don't do it all at once and freak out.

Eventually, you might want to give your parents another chance. Be careful. They may respond positively, or they may try to squash your aliveness and put you down. Whichever way they respond, don't take it too seriously. Their expectations of you say more about them than about what you should do.

You might benefit from the support of a counselor as you struggle to become a feeling person. Such a person could help you deal with your fears and encourage your movement towards a richer life.

Your Parents Neglect Your Basic Needs

Darryl's family situation is bizarre, to say the least. He lives with a cranky grandfather and a mother who's unconventional. The family is very poor, and his grandfather has just gone back to work after a long lay-off. Darryl's mother is forever trying to raise money, but she goes about it in weird and futile ways. For instance, one time she decided to raise and sell rabbits. She didn't want to bother with cages, so dozens of untrained baby rabbits had the run of the house. Darryl's mother eventually sold most of the animals, but in the meantime there were messes everywhere.

Darryl was very embarrassed about his smelly, rundown home. He also felt miserable because he had few clothes and hole-ridden tennis shoes. He never knew for sure whether there would be food in the house and rarely had a meal cooked for him. Depressed about his family life, he often contemplated suicide as a way out.

Fortunately, his mother took Darryl to a counselor when

his depression got bad. When he started feeling better, Darryl landed an excellent job after school and used the money to start buying himself clothes. He also stayed away from home as much as possible, studying at the library and hanging out at friends' homes. Interestingly, Darryl was offered several foster homes but turned them down.

If your parents are not providing the basics for you—food, shelter, and clothing—then you and your family need assistance. If your parents are incapable of getting that help because of alcoholism, depression, or mental illness, you may be the only one together enough to do it.

Where do you start? The best place is your school counselor or principal. Although it's embarrassing to reveal the mess your family's in, these people will not think less of you. They will want to help, and they know whom to contact about getting your family financial aid. If you prefer, you can call the appropriate agency yourself. Look in the phone book under United States Government. Under that heading you should find a listing for Department of Social Services or Welfare. The operator can also help you get the right number for a local or state agency that can assist your family.

Your Parent is an Alcoholic

Living with an alcoholic parent means living with stress—stress that comes at you from a dozen directions. Uncertainty is constant: is he or she going to come home drunk or sober? Will the house be clean when you get home from school or will the dishes still be in the sink and gin bottles strewn around the living room? Is there going to be a scene tonight or will things be somewhat normal?

Bringing friends home—or having friends at all—feels risky. You can't trust your alcoholic parent. You never know what condition he or she will be in. It's not only embarrassing if she's drunk, but everybody at school might find out. Consequently, you've probably learned to be very choosy about whom you trust. Your friendships may be strained further by the part of you that's jealous: you'd give anything to have a "normal" family like those of your friends.

Stress rips through your family relationships, too. You feel torn about your alcoholic parent. Loving him sometimes, hating him at others. You want to help but know you are helpless. Your mother see-saws between fierce loyalty to your father and threats of divorcing him. When she's mad at your father, she wants you to be mad at him, too. But your anger doesn't always coincide with hers, so she gets mad at you.

Sometimes it feels as if the whole family chooses sides. Your father has his pet, your mother hers. That sets you and your siblings against each other. Yet you pull together when Dad gets drunk because he's so impossible to deal with. His verbal attacks devastate you. Your self-esteem is shaky, and you worry that he may be right about your shortcomings. Maybe you *are* no good, you wonder secretly.

How on earth do you cope with such a chaotic life? Trying to answer this question, two teenage children of alcoholics—Paul Dolmetsch and Gail Mauricette—got together and wrote a wonderful book. *Teens Talk About Alcohol and Alcoholism* (Doubleday, 1987). In it they wrote about the choices kids of alcoholics have, even though it often seems as though they have none. The following discussion includes some of their advice:

1. Never argue with a drunk: leave drunken parents alone, ignore them. They don't know what they're doing, and they get upset easily. They also stick to their side of stories no matter what facts you have, because they're sure they are right.

2. When your parent is drunk, go to your room or call a friend. If you can, avoid being in the house so that you won't get beaten or injured if your parent loses control.

Go to a relative's house, a friend's house, take a drive (drive carefully), take a walk, or ride your bike. Liz, a teenager neighbor of mine, used to sleep in our hammock when her mother went on drunken rampages. Things usually didn't get crazy until about two in the morning, and Liz didn't want to wake our family. So she'd just grab her pillow and blanket and head over to our porch.

3. Get outside help. Instead of thinking you can handle the problem alone, enlist some help. The best would be getting an alcohol specialist involved. Most private and public mental health agencies have people who specialize in alcoholism. Just call up and tell the receptionist you have an alcoholic parent and would like to talk to somebody. Adults are extremely sympathetic to kids in alcoholic families, and they'll bend over backward to help you. Many hospitals now have alcohol abuse programs, too, so you can call the hospital and ask to speak to a counselor from that program.

Al-Anon and Alateen are groups associated with Alcoholics Anonymous. They're set up especially for the family members of alcoholics. They have their own separate meetings where they talk about coping with alcoholics. Everyone in the group has the same problem, so you don't have to feel weird or embarrassed. Going to a meeting may be awkward for you the first time. If you feel shy and embarrassed, that's okay. You don't have to talk. You can just listen. As an intermediate step you can call Alateen and ask to have one of its teenage members call you before you go to your first meeting.

Another source of help is your local Suicide and Crisis hotline. They have trained people who will be glad to talk to you about any subject that's bothering you. You don't have to be suicidal to call.

4. If you live in an alcoholic family, it's vitally important to have someone to talk to. This drains away some of the pressure. Find someone you can allow yourself to trust. One way you can reassure yourself is to notice some things about the person you're thinking of confiding in. Does this person share problems with you? If so, he or she would probably be comfortable hearing yours. On the other hand, if this friend gets all weird and silly when you talk about serious stuff, you'll want to choose someone else to handle your confidences.

   Obviously, a person who gossips is not safe to talk to. You can test such a person out, though. Before you tell him what's really bothering you, tell him something trivial. See what happens to that information. If it gets all over school, he isn't trustworthy.

5. Consider finding another place to live if your family life is intolerable. Possibilities are moving in with an older brother or sister, another relative, a friend's family or to a foster home. You can find out about foster homes by talking to a school counselor or by calling a crisis hotline in your area. Another way is to look in your phone book under County Government Agencies. Then look for a subheading called Social Services, or Child Protective Services or Welfare. These agencies vary from state to state, and they can give you the right number for your area. The telephone information operator may know the right phone number, too.

6. Get away from abuse: If your alcoholic parent loses it when he or she is drunk and abuses you physically or sexually, you need to find a safe place for yourself. That may mean moving out. If you can't find any place to go, get help. The quickest way is to call the police, or go to the police; otherwise, tell your family doctor, minister, or therapist. Laws in almost all states re-

quire these adults to report abuse to an agency that protects kids and teenagers.

When you think about doing one of these things you probably feel guilty and worry that you're going to hurt your parent and your family. Actually, the reverse is true. Your family needs help desperately and isn't getting it. Very often a crisis helps an alcoholic. It forces that person to face the fact that he or she is out of control, that alcohol is ruining his or her life. So getting help for yourself helps everyone.

Your Parents Don't Get Along

When your parents argue a lot, or when there is a lot of tension between them, your home life can be miserable. It was for Cora.

Cora's parents alternated between affection and explosive arguments. After an argument, her parents refused to talk to each other. A cold war was on. An only child, Cora was especially affected by the tension between her parents. In desperation she'd act as an amateur marriage counselor and often succeeded in getting her parents talking to each other again. Although Cora's parents benefited from her efforts, she didn't. She ended up feeling much too responsible for conflicts she didn't create and couldn't control. Eventually she developed stomach problems.

If you find yourself in Cora's situation, your best bet is to stay as clear of your parents' problems as you can. Involving yourself makes it awfully hard not to take sides or end up angry at one parent. That anger can cause you some guilt, which you don't need. Let your parents handle their problems. You have enough to deal with just being an adolescent.

If their fights just drag on, month in and month out, and you dread going home, tell your parents how you feel. Ask them to get outside help—if not for themselves, at least for you and your sisters and brothers. Otherwise, it probably makes sense for you to keep busy and stay away from home as much as you can. Perhaps you can get involved in after-school activities, get a part-time job, go to the library at night, or study at a friend's house. In other words, stay away from home in a productive and safe way.

Your Parents Are Divorced

Many excellent books are available to help you cope with your parents' divorce. To ward off depression, it's important to keep a few things in mind. If your parents were divorced recently, it's important to let yourself feel sad and unhappy. Don't try to be cool and brave. No matter how old you are, it hurts when parents split up. If it happened when you were younger, you may have some leftover feelings bothering you, which are discussed in Chapter 2.

If your parents continue to fight, try to protect yourself from their stress by not taking sides. If one parent wants to bad-mouth the other, ask him or her not do do that in front of you. Hearing critical things about a parent can make you feel a little down about yourself. If your mother asks you to deliver a messge to your father, or vice versa, gently refuse. Carrying messages can put you right in the middle of their disputes. If your parents fight frequently, your whole family might benefit from counseling.

Chapter Twelve

A Better Social Life

Teenagers don't like lots of things about themselves. What they don't like ranges from their stubby fingernails to their entire personalities. Unfortunately, such self-criticism can lead to lousy self-esteem, and that sets in motion a whole merry-go-round of consequences. If you figure everyone else thinks you're a nerd, too, you may feel self-conscious and shy. The shyer you act, the harder it is to make friends. The fewer friends you have, the lonelier you are, and the more you feel like an outcast. Your self-esteem sinks even further, and you can grow depressed. When you're depressed it's hard to *move,* much less do anything to help yourself feel better.

How to Like Yourself More

You aren't down on yourself because something's uniquely screwed up about you. Being self-critical is usually part of being a teenager. Covering up and trying to appear self-confident is also normal, but since everyone else is also faking it, you may feel like the only one with problems. The ironic thing is that even the most popular people in your school—the jocks, cheerleaders, class officers, and prom princesses—

feel insecure in some areas. "Naw," you're probably thinking, "Not them. How could they? They've got everything!"

Well, like you, they expect perfection of themselves and so they're never satisfied. And the class structure in junior and senior high school is one of the most rigid in society. A person would have to search hard to find another environment that's riddled with so many tight little groups. And these cliques aren't exactly friendly and welcoming; they can be full of critical, gossipy, and snobby people. Five percent of the people are "in," which leaves ninety-five percent with a golden opportunity for feeling lousy about themselves.

Even though your social environment undermines confidence, you can still do many things to feel better about yourself:

1. Notice when you put yourself down and engage in screwy thinking (see Chapter 5). Saying critical things to yourself is habit-forming and these putdowns may begin to seem like the truth eventually. So, when you scold yourself, be careful to say only those things you might say to a friend.

2. Praise yourself for your efforts, not just for your successes. This one's harder than it sounds. People tend to see things as either successful or not, and don't always notice anything in between. You hear this kind of talk all the time during pro football season. The coaches and players say things like, "It doesn't matter how well any one game goes, man. All that matters is the results. You either make it all the way or you don't." The inference is clear. Anything less than making it to the Super Bowl doesn't count.

   If you find yourself in this "all or nothing" kind of thinking, shift your focus. If, for instance, you study hard but get a C+ on a test, focus on the fact that you gave up some free time and really worked hard. You also learned a lot; it's just that what you learned didn't completely match what was on the test.

3. Rather than comparing yourself to other people, pay attention to your own strengths and assets. There is always someone who is prettier, smarter, faster, or funnier than we are. It's just too depressing to have to look at that fact every day. Every time you catch yourself feeling envious of another person, say to yourself: "Yes, he does have bigger pecs, but I _____." Keep the compliment ledger balanced between yourself and others.

4. If you can't think of anything you like about yourself now, think back to something you have liked in the past or are looking forward to in the future. If you used to like your smile, for instance, what happened? Braces? Visualize how terrific you're going to look when they're off. If you just can't picture it, think about a friend who's gotten hers off. Your looks will improve just as much. Maybe more. If you still can't think of one measly thing to like about yourself, ask a friend what he or she likes about you. Really listen and try to let the positives get through your alligator skin! Then, when you're by yourself, remember those compliments and luxuriate in them. They're true.

5. Review your decision-making skills. Think about the good choices you've made. Re-read the chapters on decision-making and problem-solving. Every time you make a good decision, your self-esteem will go up.

6. Look at each of your shoulders to make sure there isn't a chip sitting there. Those chips make it easy to distort neutral comments into negative ones. One of the unfortunate parts of human nature is that when we're down on ourselves, we expect everyone else to be, too. Consequently, we miss good feelings coming our way or twist them to match our moods.

7. Make distinctions in your mind between "I think" and "I know." When you get the two confused, it's very easy to make faulty assumptions and get yourself in a mess.

8. Be aware of your expectations. Setting your standards so high that you won't be able to meet them is a sure way to get depressed.

9. When you set a goal, break it down into steps that you can accomplish one by one. If you get two out of ten steps done, congratulate yourself. If you can go on and reach your goal, terrific. If not, set it aside. You can always go back to it later. Or you can forget it. Something better may come along.

If You're Shy and Lonely

When you start liking yourself better, you'll feel more self-confident. Talking to people gets easier, but it doesn't always happen quickly. Until it does, you may still feel trapped by your shyness and isolation. It may seem to you that you're the only one who's lonely, but one researcher has found that teenage girls are the loneliest people in our society.

Breaking out of your isolation takes a bit of reading and a bit of planning. Like all goals, this is best achieved a step at a time. Begin by reading the chapters in this book called "How to Get Close to People" and "How to Be Assertive." Before you start your campaign, here are a couple of tips you can use right away.

Shy people tend to look down when they're walking. Even if their heads are up, they quickly look down or away when they see another person coming their way. If you're like this, try to start looking at other people instead of ducking. This says you're willing to make contact. You can help distract yourself from feeling awkward by focusing on the other person. What color are her eyes? What kind of nose does he have?

Practice this with just one person a day at first. A few days later, add another person. This sounds like such an easy thing to do, but it takes courage to hang in there and look straight at someone. Whenever you do it, praise yourself. Looking at people is an important step in getting over shyness.

Not looking at people sends all the wrong messages. The people you're avoiding don't think, "Oh, she's just shy." Instead, they may decide, "What a snob. Isn't she cold?" Or, "Who does he think he is?"

When you've been able to look at people comfortably for a few weeks, begin acknowledging their smiles. When you kept your head down, you missed it when people smiled at you or looked friendly. Now that you've got your eyes up, you'll notice that other people are seeking contact, too. Nod your head in response. Think a smile. Even if it doesn't reach your mouth, it will show in your expression. In time, start smiling with your mouth. At first it may feel risky and scary. All the more reason to pat yourself on the back when you've been able to use new behaviors.

Shy people are fairly sensitive to rejection. Try not to feel overly discouraged if you smile at someone and get a scowl or blank look in return. It will take others a while to get used to the change in you. At first, they may feel puzzled by your friendliness and even a little wary. Give them time to trust you.

After you've gotten comfortable looking at people's eyes and smiling, respond when someone says, "hi." Say "hi" back or something else quick like, "How are you?"

Next, initiate saying "hi." Say it like you mean it. It usually helps to relax with a deep breath, smile, and make eye contact as you start to say hello. If you mumble it under your breath, duck your head, and scuttle away, people may not get your real message.

As you build these social skills, your confidence gradually grows. What may seem impossible when you just read about it, will seem more natural if you actually get into gear and do these things. The next step is getting a conversation going. Before you do this, study the people around you. How do they go about starting conversations and keeping them going? You can learn tons just by watching. In addition, here are some suggestions to get you started:

1. Request help. "Do you know where room L13 is? I never heard of it."

2. Compliment something about the other person. "I like that outfit," or "You did really well on that test."

3. Fall back on some familiar openers: "Boy, the snow's really coming down hard. I wonder if the game will be cancelled?"

4. Say something about yourself. "I'm completely confused about what we're supposed to do for this project."

Once you've gotten a conversation started, then what do you do? How do you keep it going?

1. Ask a question. It can be factual, such as, "How'd Cincinnati do in the playoffs?" or personal, "What do you think about the mess on Student Council?"

2. Get the other person talking about him or herself. Let's say you're at a school dance and this guy asks you to dance. You don't know him well, but you think he's cute. You could tell him you haven't seen him around a lot before and then ask him who he hangs around with, or what he does after school. Most people love talking about themselves. They're confident about doing it because they know themselves. They don't have to worry about looking stupid.

3. React to what people tell you. Use their statements as

a launching pad to ask more questions or to tell them something about yourself.

You're entitled to feel satisfied and proud if you have even short conversations at first. Each time you'll find your self-confidence rising and your skills improving. If things go badly now and then, don't give up. Learning to talk comfortably to people takes lots of practice. Don't expect to be good at it right away.

Listening Is Important, Too

Even when you get over your shyness, you may discover you're just not a big talker. You may enjoy listening as much as you do talking. Every talker needs a listener, so you will bring something valuable to each conversation. In fact, being a good, attentive listener is as much of a social asset as being a great talker.

Looking at most relationships, you'll notice that one person in the couple is talkative, the other quieter. Part of why they're drawn to each other is that they balance out. If they both talked like magpies, neither would listen much to the other. People wouldn't want to be around them, either, because they'd drive everyone crazy with their yakking. If you are quiet, value that in yourself. You'll be the perfect partner for someone who's more outgoing and chatty.

Making Friends

Making good friends seems to get harder as you get older. In grammar school, it was a cinch. Your friends were usually the kids who lived in your neighborhood. In junior and senior high, those neighborhood alliances don't always last. You may have to find new friends.

People your age are often judgmental about each other,

which complicates finding friends. In addition, the standards of acceptability may have far more to do with how you look than what kind of person you are. This makes it difficult, but not impossible, to make new friends.

The first step is polishing your antennae, the part of you that senses when people are making friendly overtures. Shy and self-conscious people can be so tuned in to their own nervousness, they don't pay attention to people around them. Consequently, they miss out on the chance to make friends with people who are being friendly.

So stay alert. For instance, if someone asks you whether you've seen a particular movie, he or she may be fishing to see if you want to see it with them. If you want to go, show some enthusiasm. Perhaps say something like, "No, I haven't, but I really want to. I hear it's good." Even if the movie sounds dumb, think about your response. Saying, "No, I hear it's lousy," may make other person stop right there and not ask you if you want to go. In other words, try to read between the lines a little.

In the beginning, extending gestures of friendship feels risky. Because of that, people do it in ways that feel safe, which often means in subtle ways. You'll probably feel safer, too, if you start slowly. If you have a class with someone you'd like as a friend, casually talk to that person before or after class. If he or she seems friendly, keep chatting for a couple of weeks. Then escalate it a bit. Ask if he wants to eat lunch with you, or if she wants to do something else that's happening around school. If the person says yes, and you enjoy being together, notice if he or she takes a turn at inviting you to do something. If they do, this a clear sign that the person wants to continue the process of becoming friends.

If the other person doesn't suggest an activity, call you up, or seek you out at school, it can mean two things. He or she either doesn't want to be friends, or is too shy to initiate an invitation. If you suspect it's a case of shyness, be patient. You may have to do all the asking for a while. If the other person isn't particularly shy, then you might want to back off for a while and see what happens. Not hearing from her may be a clue she doesn't want to be closer friends.

Sex

Since sex is a normal, healthy part of growing up, it's not a problem unless it's misused. Sex is misused if you do it to get other needs met or if you end up feeling crummy about yourself afterwards.

Debi is a cute, petite girl with big boobs. She lives with her divorced mother and visits her father during school holidays. Debi's mother is wrapped up in her career and frequently leaves Debi on her own. She also treats Debi more like a friend than a daughter. Debi and her mother don't argue much, but Debi feels unimportant. She longs for a "regular" family in which people are connected, close, and affectionate.

Since she was fourteen, Debi has found a sure-fire way to get attention and affection. From boys. They can't wait to get their hands on her, and she lets them. In the last three years she's had sex with about twenty guys. Sometimes she has relationships with them that last a month or two; more often she just has a few dates with each one.

At this point Debi is fed up with herself and with guys who date her just to have sex. She realizes she's never going to get what she wants—warmth and caring—by being promiscuous. Her self-esteem is in shambles, and she has no idea whether a guy will care for her on the basis of her personality. Now that she knows this, though, she's on the right track. She's going to try to get her needs met in a healthy way.

Paul misuses sex in a different way. He uses it to rebel against his strict and strait-laced father. Obsessed with morality, Paul's dad turns every discussion into a lecture about right and wrong. He also keep close tabs on Paul's every move and questions him about who he sees and where he goes. Paul hates his father's inquisitions but doesn't dare say so. If he complains, he's grounded. Paul gets even by doing the one thing he knows would drive his father to distraction: he has sex with every girl he can.

Paul's rather proud of his studly conquests, so he's not about to stop. But his method of rebelling is risky. He's not conscientious about birth control, so he's probably going to get a girl pregnant and have a huge mess on his hands—especially with his father. He also shortchanges himself and his girlfriends, especially now that the AIDS virus is such a threat, by using sex to express his anger.

Should you see some of yourself in Debi or Paul, try to uncover what it is you're really using your sexuality for. Look at your hurt and anger. Both are fertile ground for acting out feelings through sex. Think about ways you can express your feelings, or get your needs met, that will leave you with self-respect.

Homosexuality

One question that haunts teenagers, especially boys, is whether they're homosexual. It's a disturbing question, not because homosexuality is awful, but because our culture is so nasty about it. This section includes some guidelines to help you figure out if you are gay. A discussion of issues that are important to gay teenagers follows.

Are You Gay?

Sexual orientation is not a black or white thing. Instead, people fall on a continuum that ranges from heterosexual to homosexual. Approximately 90 percent of this country's (and the world's) population is heterosexual and 10 percent is homosexual. These percentages are true in the animal kingdom as well. Along the spectrum are people who are bisexual, but their bisexuality is not necessarily a fifty–fifty kind of thing. For instance, a bisexual woman may be most often attracted to men and occasionally find a woman attractive as well.

The same can be said for "straight," or heterosexual people. Ninety-nine percent of the time they're turned on by people of the opposite sex. Once in a while they'll find someone of their own sex arousing. That doesn't make them gay or even "bi," it just means that their sexual orientation is not constant every second of their lives.

This variability is easier to understand if you look at the connection between our love feelings and our sexual feelings. When we love someone who is the same sex, it's very natural for a fleeting sexual thought or feeling to accompany our love. Love and sexuality are not always separate. That very connection enriches your love for your boyfriend or girlfriend.

For instance, when people begin developing sexually, they often get tremendous crushes on people of the same sex. Those crushes may or may not have sexual thoughts connected to them. Either way, these feelings of admiration are normal for young teenagers and don't indicate homosexuality. People at this age may also have sex play with people who are the same sex. It isn't unusual for twelve-year-old boys and girls to fondle each other a bit, or for boys to have jerk-off parties.

Homosexual experiences in all-girl or all-boy boarding schools are also common. Young people are horny and if they don't have any opposite-sex partners available, they'll make do with kids of the same sex. Again, this behavior doesn't necessarily mean they're homosexual.

Homosexuals become aware of their orientation in different ways. Some know they're gay from a very early age. For others the realization comes gradually over a number of years. The first thing they may notice is that they have absolutely no sexual interest in people of the opposite sex.

Their friends may be raving about this girl's rear end or that guy's build, and they can't relate to the conversation at all. It's not that they dislike people of the opposite sex; they're just not even mildly attracted.

Because that feels weird and worrisome, some people fake it—to themselves and to other kids. One gay man, Bill, described taking a girl to the prom. "I had a good time and everything. It wasn't that. But I just wasn't interested. I tried kissing her but that didn't do anything either. I just didn't feel a thing."

Besides a lack of interest in the opposite sex, slowly or suddenly a gay teenager finds himself or herself turned on to people of the same sex. Bill found himself getting erections in the locker room and tried to ignore what that meant. He went all through high school and part of college wondering whether he was gay, but he was too terrified to find out. One night, he couldn't stand it any longer and decided he had to know. He drove over to a gay bar, got picked up, went to bed with a guy, and loved it. (Bill's experience took place years before the onset of AIDS and the current risks of casual sex.) From then on he knew he was gay.

Looking back on his childhood, he said he was always different from the other boys. While his older brother played football, Bill's favorite activity was rearranging his mother's furniture. Today he's a talented designer.

Bill's recollection of always being different brings up an important point: researchers and psychologists currently believe that homosexuality is primarily determined at birth. In other words, it's genetically determined, just like brown hair or blue eyes. So homosexuals may not have any choice about their sexual orientation. If you stop to think about it, that makes a lot of sense. For most people sexual attraction to another person either exists or doesn't. It's not something we can talk ourselves into unless we're very, very needy sexually. Nor are we usually successful at talking ourselves out of finding someone attractive. On the whole, sexual attraction isn't a matter of control. It's just a spontaneous feeling.

Perhaps you have had this experience. Someone you know and like very much asks you out on a date. You go, have a good time, and yet feel nothing sexually. You're such a good match otherwise that you think things would just be perfect if you could just get turned on. So you go out a few more times to see if anything develops. Nothing happens. You don't feel a thing. Reluctantly you give up the idea of making this into a romance.

Likewise, if you are gay, the first thing to recognize is that you simply can't control chemistry. Nothing is wrong, awful, weird, or screwed up about you because you are gay. Nature has determined that 10 percent of all people and animals will be homosexual. You happen to be in that 10 percent. Try not to waste your energy blaming anyone—your parents, fate, or yourself.

At the same time, being a minority in our society is hell. There's no point in pretending otherwise. It's especially tough for a teenager because you naturally want to feel that you belong, that you're like everyone else. You might find it helpful to remind yourself of two things. First, you are very much like the majority of other teens in every respect but one. Differing in this way doesn't make you an outcast, a freak.

Second, if you are a male you are every bit as masculine as your heterosexual friends. Masculinity does not mean making love to women. The dictionary describes "masculine" primarily as being male. You qualify there. Then it mentions strength, vigor, and sexual potency. To what degree that fits you depends on your muscles, energy, and sex drive. It has nothing to do with your sexual orientation.

A "female" is one who "brings forth young or produces ova." In other words, someone who has babies or ovulates is defined as being "feminine." (Interestingly, the dictionary I have doesn't give any more clues to femininity other than technical references to biology and being able to accept male electrical plugs! A sexist dictionary for sure.)

Remember, too, that you are not the only one in your school who's gay. Every tenth person walking down the hall is also gay. You are not alone, even though you probably feel different and isolated. If you haven't told anyone you're gay, you may feel you're dragging around an enormous boulder everywhere you go. Unloading your secret will be freeing, but you'll want to do it in a way that's safe.

Whom should you tell? The ideal person would be someone who isn't judgmental about homosexuals, someone who can keep secrets and who has shared one of his or her troubles with you. This person may be a friend, counselor, or perhaps a brother or sister. If you have a number of people who know you're gay and support you, you won't be left high and dry if something happens to any one confidant.

Finding that support system takes time. You may be able to find other gay kids in your school. If not, then see if you can find a rap group for gay people in your community. You can call a local crisis line and talk to a counselor by phone. This person will ask you your first name, but that's all. If you like, you can even use a different name. You can stay anonymous and talk freely about anything that's bothering you.

Whether to tell your parents can be a wrenching issue. The answer depends a lot on how you read them. No matter how liberal and understanding they are, it's realistic to expect that they will be upset, at least for a while. Out of ignorance and guilt they may wonder what they've done wrong. They may also worry about you and your future happiness. To put it another way, they will need some time to process your news. You've probably taken a number of years to get used to your homosexuality, and your parents may take about as long to accept it.

On the other hand, many parents of gays have said they wish their kids had told them years sooner. These parents suspected their kids were gay but never knew for sure. They hated not knowing. But then, they didn't ask.

If you think your parents can handle the truth without doing great emotional damage to *you*, you might want to tell them. Perhaps they can become a source of support. If, however, your parents are rigid, judgmental, self-righteous, and have very set rules about what is moral and virtuous, they may not handle your news well. Wait until you're older and decide then whether to tell them.

Once you're through high school, you'll probably find life much easier. If you choose to, you can be more open about your homosexuality. Some people will still be shocked, but most will be far more tolerant and less threatened than the kids in high school. Other choices will open up to you as well. If you seem to be the only gay in town, you can move to a community that has a larger gay population. If you go away to college, you'll find that many campuses have gay student organizations.

Just like your heterosexual counterparts, you'll have opportunities to fall in love and settle down in a committed relationship. You can buy a house, advance in your career, have satisfying hobbies and activities. Being gay in no way dooms you to a secretive, unsettled life of cruising bars. Many homosexuals live very average lives. So average, in fact, you can't tell them from the other people on the block.

Chapter Thirteen

Getting Closer to People

Two juniors are standing in line at their high school snack bar. Sarah turns around in line to talk to Jennie:

"How are you? I haven't seen you in a while."

"Yeah, I know. Fine. Uh, how are you?"

"Fine, really great."

"Gee, that's great, really good."

Sarah and Jennie have just had a superficial, but safe conversation. Since neither girl disclosed a morsel of truth about herself, neither feels vulnerable or exposed. But they both left the conversation feeling detached and empty. If they had trusted each other, Jennie might have responded to Sarah's question with,

"Yeah, I know. Things have been the pits. John and I broke up, and I've been hating life."

"You too! I found out that Steve's been messing around with that sleaze Melody."

"No kidding. They're all like that."

When we trust each other, we can be honest about our lives and feelings. In this second conversation, Jennie and Sarah might have felt closer to each other and also proud that they had been entrusted with such personal information.

They might also have felt less alone: neither was the only one with boy troubles.

Sarah and Jennie's honesty with each other is called self-disclosure—telling another person something personal about yourself. If you're an average teenager, the idea of opening up probably raises at least a few reservations. "Ha, never!" you may say to yourself. "There's no way I would do that. They'd laugh at me, or it would get all over school."

Your reluctance is understandable. The name of the game in junior and senior high is not openness and self-expression but self-protection. Being seen as weird or different is so deadly that most teens hide their feelings and cover up their individuality. They feel safer behind masks because the masks make it easier to fit in with other people. Some wear jock masks, others brain masks, friendly Miss-Popular masks, and hard-ass masks. As different as these masks appear, they all serve the same purpose: they hide the scared, insecure person who wants to be liked and accepted.

Why Risk It?

Why should a person consider taking off the mask and revealing personal stuff? For starters, our masks cover less than we might think because our bodies give us away. Facial expression, posture, tone of voice, and even a little sigh all reveal how we really feel, no matter how hard we try to cover it up.

Suppose you're angry at your best friend, but you're not ready to talk about it. When you see him, you try to act like everything's fine, but you avoid looking him in the eye. He can tell you're mad about something, but he doesn't know what. He gets defensive and acts cold and distant. Your friendship's quickly in a mess—all because you hoped you could cover up your feelings.

Another reason to share feelings is that it will help you know yourself better. Unspoken thoughts and feelings often remain vague and cloudy. Talking about them requires putting them in some sort of order so that others can understand them. This process helps you get a sharper fix on what you feel.

Sometimes we don't know all our feelings. Imagine yourself yakking away to a friend and suddenly saying something you didn't even know you felt. Unconscious feelings like this often surface more quickly in conversation than when we are alone. Since these feelings help us know ourselves better, that is another benefit of talking about ourselves.

Sharing your feelings also encourages close and deep relationships. This is called intimacy. If you haven't learned how to be intimate, you may feel lonely even though you have several friends. This loneliness comes from playing it too safe—keeping your talk light and superficial and avoiding closeness.

Still another advantage of talking about your feelings is getting rid of "the guilties." When you tell someone that you feel terrible about a thought you've had or something you've done, you accomplish two things. First, you stop hiding it, which lightens your guilt load. Second, you can look at your "sin" far more objectively. It may turn out that your supposedly rotten act or hideous thought is perfectly average and normal. Having another person tell you this is one of the quickest ways to discover you're not alone.

How To Do It

Learning to be open with another person is a three-step process. You can ease into it at a comfortable pace, take as long as you need to learn each step, and move to the next one only when you feel ready. This isn't a crash course in spilling your guts.

Step 1. If you are able to self-disclose with your close friends and family, go on to practice these steps with people you know less well. This will give you better practice in deepening relationships with new people in your life. On the other hand, if it's hard for you to be open with friends, then practice with people you're at ease with, like members of your family. When you're comfortable, then you can begin using your new skills with friends.

After you've decided who you want to practice on, begin by telling him or her a safe, impersonal *fact* about yourself; leave out your thoughts or feelings. You can easily slip a fact into a conversation the same way you would a comment on the weather. Just blurt it out. It won't seem strange or awkward at all. You might say something like:

"I just took old man Barstow's history test," or "Yeah, we rode that same ferry when we went to Victoria."

When you feel comfortable revealing facts about yourself, it's time to move on to the next step.

Step 2. To reveal a little more about yourself, talk about the thoughts, feelings, and needs you've had in the past or that you're expecting in the future:

"I'm supposed to take the S.A.T. Saturday. It's the second time I've taken it. The first time I didn't do too well, and I felt like a nerd."

Step 3. Ultimately, you begin talking about what you want, need, or feel at the moment. Often this will have something to do with the person you're talking to, so it may take practice—and courage. Fortunately, this way of talking can resolve major situations. Let's say you finally get an opportunity to talk to someone you've been attracted to for ages. This is your big moment, but you're nervous, you freeze up. Now what? Instead of making a quick getaway, you say, "I've been wanting to meet you and now I can't think of a thing to say."

Chances are the person has been through the same experience. Your honesty and poise may charm and intrigue him or her. By being honest, you've turned a potential disaster into something quite positive.

You'll notice that this last statement was far more interesting and lively than the things said in Steps 1 and 2. That's because the person in the third example was letting you in on his humanness, his feelings. People find other people's feelings fascinating, even yours!

You'll also be relieved to know that people rarely criticize feelings. They may not always agree with them, or quite understand them, but they're not apt to be mean about how other people feel. Nor are they likely to gossip about feelings. Behavior is much juicier gossip material. You've probably never overheard someone say in a scandalized voice, "Did you know that she got nervous before her date!" No, what she did on her date makes much better gossip. So don't let fear of being criticized or talked about stop you from sharing your feelings. You'll find that people like you better, not less.

Chapter Fourteen

A Friend Who's Seriously Depressed

Teenagers rarely reveal their depression in the same way as adults. They may not act unhppy or say they're depressed. That makes it confusing when you think something is wrong with a teenage friend or relative. For instance, your friend used to be outgoing and peppy, and lately she's quiet and tired all the time. Should you be concerned?

In general, trust your instincts. If you can't quite put your finger on what's changed, it doesn't matter. Your intuitive concern is all the evidence you need to follow up on. Many parents and friends of teenagers who have attempted or completed suicide have said, "I thought something wasn't quite right, but I didn't know for sure. I wish I had said something or done something." So, trust your sense of alarm. If it turns out you're wrong and the person's fine, that's okay. As a caring human being you took a risk on behalf of your friend's life.

Although teens often mask their depression (see Chapter 4), their behavior almost always changes when their depression worsens, or when they're considering suicide. Generally, change in just one area, such as sleep, doesn't necessarily indicate depression. It can just be a transitory mood or behavior change. If behavior changes in two or three areas and stays changed for two weeks or more, it's more likely depression. Things to watch out for are:

1. Personality changes: seems down, listless, quiet.
2. Increased hopelessness and helplessness: says things like, "What's the point of living?" "It all stinks, you can't change anything."
3. Increased anger: lashes out for no apparent reason.
4. Withdrawal from family and friends: begins spending a lot of time alone.
5. Cries frequently and easily.
6. Talks about suicide or makes remarks about wanting to sleep forever.
7. Sleep patterns change. Wakes up in the middle of the night or early morning, and can't go back to sleep.
8. Can't concentrate.
9. Spends hours and hours watching TV.
10. Personal habits deteriorate: clothes are dirty, room is more of a mess.
11. Loses interest in activities he or she used to enjoy.
12. Eating habits change: can't eat or overeats.

The following behaviors are serious indications that your friend may be considering suicide:

1. Acts more impulsively than ever before and takes many more risks.
2. Has been depressed and all of a sudden, for no reason, acts happy. (He or she may just be relieved because he has made the decision to commit suicide.)

3. Tells you he or she's thinking about committing suicide.

4. Starts giving away prized possessions.

How to Respond to Depression

If you have a friend who is depressed and you're worried she may be suicidal, ask her. You won't be putting ideas into her head or increasing the risk of her doing it. If she says, "No, it's something I've thought about, but would never do," you can relax a bit. Encourage her to talk as much as she can, though, about what's bothering her. Avoid trying to cheer her up and show her the bright side of her problems. That usually backfires because the depressed person feels you're not really listening. If you truly understood, she believes, you would see how painful her life is.

At the same time, listening well doesn't mean you have to agree with her feelings of hopelessness. You can say something like, "Yes, I can see why you feel so awful. I'd feel terrible in that situation, too. But, I'm not sure it will stay bad forever." If you can see a partial or whole solution to your friend's problem, don't just blurt it out. She may not be able to hear it, and again, will feel misunderstood. Instead, ask her if she'd be interested in hearing your idea about what to do. If she says no, try to accept it. Try again another day, but don't push your solutions.

It is crucial that your friend get professional counseling either from your school counselor or from a licensed therapist (family counselor, psychologist, social worker, or psychiatrist). Offer to help her find a counselor, make the appointment, and even go with her. If nagging is the only way to get her to a professional, then nag.

If your friend refuses professional help, then encourage her to call your local Suicide and Crisis Hot Line. They have trained volunteers who can help. If she is too shy or embarrassed to make the call, make it with her. They can also help you. You're in a tough situation and perhaps could use their advice and support.

Breaking a Confidence

If your friend has told you she is thinking of killing herself and swears you to secrecy, you're in a bind. You don't want to violate her trust, but you're worried. What should you do? *Always, in every case*, break that confidence and tell an adult— your parent, her parent, a teacher, the principal, or the school counselor. If that adult doesn't seem concerned, keep talking until you find one who does. Your first loyalty is to your friend's life and *then* to your friendship. If your friend gets mad at you for telling, that is a small price if you save her life. Later, she'll be grateful *and* alive.

What to Do in a Crisis

If you are with a friend and you're afraid he'll kill himself as soon as you leave, don't leave. Stay with him, but call an adult to come help you. If you can't reach an adult you know, call 911 or the operator. Tell them what's going on and they will get help to you.

Bibliography

Battle, Phyllis. "Carol Burnett: What I've learned About Myself." *Ladies Home Journal*, November 1986.

Baum, Joanne. *One Step Over the Line*. New York: Harper and Row, 1985.

Bayard, Robert T. and Jean Bayard. *How to Deal with Your Acting Up Teenager*. San Jose, California: Accord Press, 1981.

Beck, Aaron T. *Cognitive Therapy and the Emotional Disorders*. New York: American Library, 1976.

Behr, Andrea. "Gay Teens Often Turn to Suicide." *San Jose Mercury News*. July 20, 1986.

Blume, Judy. *It's Not the End of the World*. New York: Bantam Books, 1972.

Cantwell, Dennis and Gabrielle Carlson. *Affective Disorders in Childhood and Adolescence. An Update*. New York: Spectrum Publications, 1983.

Cramer, Leonard. *Up From Depression*. New York: Pocket Books, 1969.

Davis, Martha, Mathew McKay, and Elizabeth Eshelman. *The Relaxation and Stress Reduction Workbook*. Richmond, California: New Harbinger Publications, 1980.

De Curtis, Anthony. "The Rolling Stone Interview with Billy Joel," *Rolling Stone*. November 6, 1986.

Dolmetsch, Paul and Gail Mauricette. *Teens Talk About Alcohol and Alcoholism*. New York: Doubleday, 1987.

Getzoff, Ann and Carolyn McClenahan. *Stepkids: A Survival Guide for Teenagers in Stepfamilies*. New York: Walker, 1984.

Giovarcchini, Peter. *The Urge to Die: Why Young People Commit Suicide*. New York: Macmillan, 1981.

Glen, Stephen H. and Joel W. Warner. *Developing Capable Young People*. Hurst Texas: Humansphere, Inc., 1985

Horrocks, John E. *The Psychology of Adolescence*. 4th ed. Boston: Houghton Mifflin Co., 1976.

Hubner, John. "A Positive Addiction." *West* Magazine. *San Jose Mercury News*, October 5, 1986.

Inoff-Germain, Gale, et al. *Relations Between Hormone Levels and Observational Measures of Aggressive Behavior of Young Adolescents in Family Interactions*. Bethesda, Maryland: National Institute of Mental Health, 1986.

Klagsburn, Francine. *Too Young To Die*. New York: Pocket Books, 1981.

Kotulak, Ronald. "The Growing Pitfalls of Adolescence." *San Jose Mercury News*, 1986.

Madison, Arnold. *Suicide and Young People*. New York: Houghton Mifflin Books, 1970.

Manaster, Guy. *Adolescent Development and the Life Tasks*. Boston: Allyn and Gacon, 1977.

McCoy, Kathleen. *Coping with Teenage Depression*. New York: Signet Books, 1982.

McKay, Mathew, Martha Davis and Patrick Fanning. *Messages, The Communication Skills Book*. Oakland: New Harbinger Publications, 1983.

Miller, Derek. *The Age Between: Adolescence and Therapy*. New York: Jason Aronson, 1983.

Mothner, Ira and Alan Weitz. *How to Get Off Drugs*. New York: Rolling Stone Press, 1984.

Ormsby, Kathy, Dale Ormsby, and Sallie Ormsby. "In Their Own Words: My Faith Has Been More Real Than Ever." *Charlotte Observer*, December 21, 1986.

Rinzler, Jane. *Teens Speak Out*. New York: Donald Fine, Inc., 1985.

Rubin, Theodore. *Overcoming Indecisiveness*. New York: Avon Books, 1985.

Schwab, Gary. "Biggest Race for Distance Runner May Be Against Self." *Charlotte Observer*, June 8, 1986.

Simon, Nissa. *Don't Worry, You're Normal*. New York: Thomas Y. Crowell, 1982.

Sorensen, Tom. "Paralyzed Track Star Tells Her Story: Fear of Failing God Led to Leap from Bridge." *Charlotte Observer*, December 21, 1986.

———. "Their Vigil Goes On, In a Hospital's Waiting Room." *Charlotte Observer*, June 9, 1986.

Stearn, Marshall. *Drinking and Driving*. Sausalito: Park West Publishing Co., 1985.

Stearns, Ann Kaiser. *Living Through A Personal Crisis*. Chicago, Illinois: The Thomas Moore Association, 1983.

Toma, David and Ira Levy. *Toma Tells It Straight with Love*. New York: Jan Publishing, 1981.

Ubell, Earl. "Is That Child Bad or Depressed?" *Parade Magazine*, November 2, 1986.

Wegscheider, Sharon. *Another Chance, Hope and Health for the Alcoholic Family*. Menlo Park: Science and Behavior Books, 1981.

Wurtman, Judith with Margaret Danbrot. "Mood Foods to Raise Your Energy or Lower Your Stress." *Redbook Magazine*, February 1987.

Youngs, Bettie B. *Stress in Children: How to Recognize, Avoid and Overcome It*. New York: Arbor House, 1985.

———. *A Stress Management Guide for Young People*. Del Mar: Bilicki Publications, 1986.

Zimbargo, Phillip. *Shyness: What It Is, What to Do About It*. New York: Jove Books, 1977.

Index